Additional Praise for *Interreligious Learning and Teaching*

"Largen, Hess, and Sapp have put their finger on the leading topic in faith forma-tion in the twenty-first century. Not only are all communities, even households, affected by the increasingly interreligious landscape of multicultural America—we still need better tools for engaging the religious other in transformative ways. This text presents comparative theology and other paradigms for interreligious engage-ment in an engaging and accessible manner. It's like joining a conversation already going on between Christians on how they have been learning to encounter inter-religious contexts in ways that transform their own faith and the faith of those they encounter."

Clint Schnekloth, Lead Pastor
Good Shepherd Lutheran Church, Fayetteville, Arkansas

"Navigating religious diversity is one of the most pressing and transformative chal-lenges of our time. Grounded in their rich experience of teaching and ministry, the authors reflect on the practical challenges and possibilities opened up by encoun-ters with followers of other religious paths. This is a thoughtful and discerning guide for all Christians interested in exploring interreligious relationships in light of the best contemporary educational practices."

Leo D. Lefebure
Georgetown University

"In *Interreligious Learning and Teaching*, Kristin Johnston Largen, Mary E. Hess, and Christy Lohr Sapp recognize the urgent need for interreligious dialogue and have provided a suggestive text, which attends with care to the pluralistic world of religious 'others' in which we live. This work calls Christians to engage that world through creative reading of the Bible and the Christian tradition, which 'walks the line between holy envy and misappropriation' of another's tradition. The text will challenge the reader to think in deeper ways about what she or he would appropriate or refuse to appropriate from the teachings and practices of the religious 'others.'"

Winston D. Persaud
Wartburg Theological Seminary

Interreligious Learning and Teaching

A Christian Rationale for Transformative Praxis

Kristin Johnston Largen

with

Mary E. Hess
Christy Lohr Sapp

INTERRELIGIOUS LEARNING AND TEACHING
A Christian Rationale for a Transformative Praxis

Cover image: Three people chatting © Marie Bertrand/Corbis
Cover design: Laurie Ingram
Book design: PerfecType, Nashville, TN

Library of Congress Cataloging-in-Publication Data is available
Print ISBN: 978-1-4514-8877-7
eBook ISBN: 978-1-4514-8969-9

The paper used in this publication meets the minimum requirements of American National Standard for Information Sciences — Permanence of Paper for Printed Library Materials, ANSI Z329.48-1984.

Manufactured in the U.S.A.

Contents

3 Outcomes, Strategies, and Assessment for Interreligious Teaching and Learning

Acknowledgments

Personally, I have never collaborated on a book like this before, with this sort of format, and honestly, I wasn't sure what to expect when Mary Hess and Christy Lohr Sapp contributed their voices. How would it all come together? How would our voices harmonize?

Well, reading over the finished product, it seems to me that this is another great example of the whole being more than the sum of its parts; and evidence as to how collaboration makes almost any individual effort stronger. I am so grateful for their work, and it is clear to me how their insights and expertise have made the book so much stronger than anything I could have written on this topic on my own. And, even more, it's a great example of how this work of interreligious teaching and learning itself simply must be a collaborative effort: no one person can do it on his or her own—it takes a village of committed colleagues, and a whole diverse community to bring about larger educational and societal changes, as well as transformation in oneself. I feel very blessed to be a part of such a community—and if you currently aren't a part of such a community, I encourage you to go out and find one, or even create one! There are others like you, I promise.

Chapter 1

Our Interreligious Life in the Twenty-First-Century North American Context

Kristin Johnston Largen

"How Interreligious Is Your Life?"

What's your experience with interreligious dialogue? That's the question I first thought I wanted to address in the opening pages of this book, but as I contemplated it more, I realized that there is an even more fundamental question that conveys much more clearly and directly the reality in which we live today: "How interreligious is your life?" That is the first question we need to be asking—both of ourselves and of the people in our churches, and, of course, of people in theological education. The main reason for beginning with this particular question is that when you ask people if they are engaged in "interreligious dialogue," the first response for many is to say "no": many Christians have never been to a synagogue, mosque, or temple, and many Christians still have few, if any, non-Christian friends. So, they don't think of themselves as actively engaging in "dialogue."

The reality, however, is that here in the United States in the twenty-first century, we all live in a pluralistic, interreligious context that marks us and shapes us in ways we sometimes don't even recognize or realize. It is naïve to assume (and narrow minded to desire) that all our children's friends, our neighbors, our doctors, and our co-workers are Christian; and there is no Internet/news bubble in which one can insulate oneself that does not include important news involving non-Christian religions.

---

*QR code URL: http://www.pluralism.org/religion.

Praxis Point #1

One of the surprising and disheartening consequences of the attacks on the World Trade Center and Pentagon in 2001 was a realization of the ignorance many Americans had around issues of the religious other. The Sikh community was among the first to experience backlash. In a 9/11 retaliatory attack, Balbir Singh Sodhi, a practicing Sikh, was gunned down while working at his gas station in Arizona.[1] He was shot by a Caucasian man who claimed to want to shoot an "Arab" and who wanted justice for Americans. Sikhs are not "Arabs"; many are Indians. Some are Caucasians, and many are also Americans. Members of the Sikh tradition have been living in the United States for over a century, and about a million Sikhs live in North America today.[2] Sikhism is the world's fifth largest religious tradition. Many Sikh men are easily identified by their long beards and turbans. The murder of Mr. Sodhi demonstrates that at the time of the 9/11 attacks many Americans did not know much about the religious other.

The Sikh community was not the only one targeted in the backlash from 9/11, and the entire interreligious landscape of the United States changed on that day. Our collective naïveté and ignorance was no longer permissible. Muslims, in particular, had a great deal of work to do to educate their neighbors about their tradition, and the place where a large portion of this education happened was in local congregations. Those who had established interreligious relationships were able to draw on those to offer words and acts of support. Those who did not suddenly found a new urgency in forming such relationships.

This all goes to show that events in one specific locale can have an impact the world over. Thus, we need an expansive understanding of the word *community*. While many individuals might not see themselves as having many interreligious relationships in their lives, that does not exclude them from participation in the wider world. My students often respond to the challenge of learning to make room for a theology of the religious other in their lives with the realization that they will be working in rural communities that are marked by homogeneity. Yet, with eyes to see, they realize that even those in rural communities watch the news or movies. Even those in homogenous communities form opinions of the "other."

As we teach people in our schools and our religious communities to reflect thoughtfully about "otherness," we teach them to become better citizens of the world. We also equip them with the skills to handle myriad types of otherness. Often, students find that the skills they learn in interreligious dialogue come in handy in awkward moments of political or ideological difference, of racial reconciliation, and gender stereotyping. In much the same way that the skills

1. For the stories, see http://religion.blogs.cnn.com/2012/08/05/10-years-after-sikh-murder-over-911
-community-continues-to-blend-in-and-stand-out/; and/or http://www.saldef.org/issues/balbir-singh
-sodhi/.
2. http://www.saldef.org/learn-about-sikhs/.

of critical thinking and articulation developed in debate serve students well in other disciplines, the particularities of listening, learning, and communicating honed in dialogue serve pastors and teachers well in many situations.—*Christy Lohr Sapp*

The fact is, our lives are marked by interreligious engagements in all kinds of ways, whether we want that to be the case or not; and consequently, as Christians, we sometimes find ourselves in situations that are confusing and leave us unsure how to respond. Therefore, it seemed wise to me to begin a book that hopes to introduce both a Christian rationale for interreligious engagement and also some concrete strategies for facilitating such an engagement with four such "situations": concrete examples of lived interreligious experiences that many of us have encountered, but to which fewer of us have consciously formulated a "proper" Christian response. And, even more, in at least one or two of the cases, it's not entirely clear what a "proper" Christian response should be, and what the grounds might be for making such a response.

So, in what follows, then, I discuss the practice of yoga, the inflammatory media stunt of Qur'an burning, Buddhist meditation, and the growing trend of "Christian" Seder meals. To be sure, there are a host of other beliefs and practices—with more coming to the fore every day, such as the Hindu festival of Holi or the Muslim observance of Ramadan—that could be addressed on the basis of their influence on North American society. However, I have selected these topics due to both their fame and infamy, as well as their ability to convey key aspects of interreligious education. Each one of these practices has its own challenges and motivations, and all of them have seen quite conflicted responses from various Christian communities. My main goal in discussing and describing each of these practices is not to make a final pronouncement either for or against (except in the case of the Qur'an burning—does anyone really want to argue *for* such a practice?), but, rather, to introduce some of the issues involved, offer some background information, and, finally, demonstrate the practical necessity for interreligious education and dialogue that seems to be of critical importance for daily life in the world today.

Praxis Point #2

What is explored here are two "categories" of potential offense in interreligious dialogue: (1) misappropriation of another's tradition, and (2) flat-out disrespect for another's tradition. The latter can easily be addressed for Christians by the Golden Rule and/or the Eighth Commandment. Jesus clearly charges his followers to treat others with the respect and dignity that they deserve as co-inhabitors of the earthly kingdom. The Eighth Commandment also challenges us to look out for the welfare of our neighbors. It does not say just to concern ourselves with our Christian neighbors. In his Small Catechism, Martin Luther expands the understanding of this commandment to include acting on the other's behalf, helping the other protect his name, his property, and his reputation. Disrespecting a person's religious tradition by maligning, abusing, or otherwise desecrating a sacred relic, text, or leader is not living into that help which Luther suggests we should offer. If anything, it does the opposite, and doing the opposite also means breaking the commandment.

In regard to the first category, often misappropriation of another's tradition can begin innocently enough. Krister Stendahl, the late Swedish Lutheran bishop, New Testament scholar, and pioneer in Lutheran-Jewish relations, encouraged people to develop "holy envy" for others' traditions. By this, he meant that we each should find something in the others' traditions that we wish we had in our own. This holy envy is a beautiful thing when it helps us to see the poetry of another's text or the piety in another's actions, but it crosses a line to misappropriation when we take that envy and turn it into imitation. While some say that imitation is the highest form of flattery, others know that imitation can actually result in just the opposite—irritation and offense. It reminds me of sibling rivalry. Nothing can annoy the older sibling more than when the younger sibling copies what she does. The younger simply wants to be like the older, but the older finds the imitation to be insulting. That is what inappropriate uses of yoga, meditation, and Seders can be. When we take elements of other traditions and try to "Christianize" them, this at its most innocent level fails to recognize the deep history of the traditions behind the elements, and, at its more sinister level, strips them of the elements of their inherent worth—suggesting that they do not have value in and of themselves as Hindu, Buddhist, Jewish, and other traditions but, rather, that they need to be "validated" by Christian patina.

We need to train our religious leaders to walk the line between holy envy and misappropriation—to draw inspiration from others without needing to claim or own those enviable aspects for themselves. Also, practioners must beware of the naïveté of thinking that because one engages in yoga, meditation, Seders, and so forth, that one "knows" Hinduism, Buddhism, or Judaism. To stereotype all Hindus as yogis or all Buddhists as master meditators is as inappropriate as suggesting that all Catholics pray the rosary or all Pentecostals speak in or have received the gift of tongues. It can be insulting to the religious other for nonadherents of the tradition to assume a familiarity that does not exist simply because he or she engages in a practice that has been removed from its original religious context. Doing yoga does not create an automatic "in" with Hindus any more than knowing the words to *Ein feste Burg* creates an automatic "in" with Germans.

In North America, in particular, the Native American traditions are another place where we would do well to exercise care not to misappropriate another's traditions. Here we also have to be especially mindful of the power dynamics at play given American history with this population and this tradition. Creating a talking circle with a designated object as the "talking piece" that designates who has the right to speak at any given time is a common technique for facilitated dialogues of many types. From leadership seminars and team-building events to recovery and reconciliation workshops, the talking circle has become a useful tool. Yet, when the method is used without acknowledging the source, is a disservice done? Perhaps there are those who would tell Native Americans that their "patent has run out" on the talking circle as a means of engaging in dialogue, but why not err on the greater side of gratitude and begin such a process with a nod to the tradition that shaped it? Could this not be a good exercise in humility, history, and remembrance?

At the 2009 Parliament of the World's Religions meeting in Melbourne, Australia, it was striking to hear every nonaboriginal Australian begin his or her remarks with a public acknowledgment of those who had "gone before": those who lived on the land before colonial occupation and those who had suffered and lost their homes, livelihoods, and identities at the hands of outsiders. This was a striking way to begin their public addresses. It represented a humility and an awareness of the interpersonal cost of colonization. What if Americans were to do this? What would that look like, and what would we say? How would we respectfully and appropriately honor the Native American communities who lost so much when settlers came to this land in search of religious freedom? How would we respectfully and appropriately honor the Africans who were brought across an ocean to help this nation prosper? How could we then more meaningfully incorporate rituals, practices, and ideas from such groups in a way that honors rather than minimizes or dismisses their contributions to modern culture? Learning to answer these questions is more than an exercise in interreligious engagement. It is also an exercise in racial reconciliation, in contrition and corporate responsibility, and in lovingkindness.—*Christy Lohr Sapp*

Yoga: Religious Practice or Physical Exercise?

Without a doubt, in the past few decades, yoga has become a cultural phenomenon. It is hardly possible to open a women's magazine without seeing a picture of this or that celebrity carrying her yoga mat pre- or post-workout (less often: "his" yoga mat), and it is the rare gym that doesn't offer a variety of yoga classes as part of a larger menu of group class options. I have practiced yoga on and off for over fifteen years, and I have experienced the full gamut of yoga studios and teachers. For example, in my current institutional context, the Lutheran Seminary in Gettysburg, Pennsylvania, we have a YWCA right on campus. It's a great facility, with excellent teachers and wonderful classes. However, the yoga teachers there also teach zumba,

Photo: Joel Nilsson. CC-by-SA 2.0 Generic license (Wikimedia Commons).

step, bootcamp, and other courses. That is, first and foremost, they are *exercise* instructors, who teach a variety of different exercise classes, of which yoga is one. The rooms, too, are all-purpose exercise rooms, with mirrors, fans in the corners, and various types of weights, mats, and the like lining the walls.

The yoga classes I have taken there are about as devoid of religious content as any I have experienced. Some of the teachers use some of the Sanskrit terms for the various poses (*asanas*): *chaturanga*, the low push-up pose, is one everyone seems to know; but many of the poses—downward-facing dog, child's pose, tree pose—always are referred to by their English names. And while the instructors certainly emphasize breathing, relaxation, focus, and even intention, none of those things are explicitly connected to a particular religious tradition. I would venture to say that absolutely anyone, of any faith, would feel comfortable taking a class there, without feeling like they were engaging in some form of religious worship or practice—and I imagine that, for the YWCA, that's intentional.

I also have taken yoga in other cities and in other studios, however, where there was much more of a focus on the Eastern religious origins of yoga, and its place in Hinduism in particular. Even in the small town of Gettysburg one can find studios and instructors in this model: there is one local yoga instructor who includes a Sanskrit *shloka* to the goddess Saraswati on the back of his business card. Typically, one finds this in dedicated yoga studios: studios whose teachers have training in the particular methods and philosophies of specific yoga masters, for example, B. K. S. Iyengar, who based his understanding of yoga on the *Yoga Sutras* of Patanjali. Sometimes, in these studios, there is explicit mention of the spiritual aspect of yoga, including teachings about enlightenment and wisdom—and some studios even have small altars with statues of Hindu gods. So, which is it: Is yoga a religious practice, which Christians in particular should avoid; or is it just another exercise that Christians would do well to try, and that even can be "Christianized" with Christian prayer and devotion? Well, of course, it's somewhere in between.

Is Yoga a Hindu Practice?

I'm sure this question has circled around in the public square more than once, but in my mind, the genesis of the most recent flurry of interest can be traced back to an event that occurred in October 2010. That month, the president of the Southern Baptist Theological Seminary in Louisville, Kentucky, Dr. Albert Mohler Jr., made headlines by calling for Christians to avoid yoga, arguing that the practice is not "a Christian pathway to God." He feels that because yoga is

A statue of the Hindu god Shiva, Bangalore, India. Photo: Kalyan Kumar. CC-by-SA 2.0 Generic license (Wikimedia Commons).

"derived from Eastern religions," it is not something that Christians should see as a spiritual practice or a means for deepening one's spiritual life. Specifically, Mohler said that he objects to "the idea that the body is a vehicle for reaching consciousness with the divine." "That's just not Christianity," Mohler said. I want to come back to Mohler's comments shortly, but first, it's worth looking at a few other public statements on this question.

    You can find the story here.[3]

Once I started digging, I saw that Mohler hadn't actually started the debate—he was responding to it. In fact, it had all begun quietly enough, with an essay on the Website for the Hindu American Foundation (HAF), and its "Take Back Yoga" campaign. The foundation had become concerned over the years that yoga has been intentionally separated from its Hindu roots, such that while yoga has a broad, deep following in the United States among people of all religions (and no religion), Hinduism itself still remains the object of misinformation, discrimination, and even scorn. For that reason, the foundation started the "Take Back Yoga" campaign, which, according to the HAF Website, really took off in November 2010, with a story in the New York *Times*.

    You can find more about "Take Back Yoga" here.[4]

The goal of the campaign, according to the article, was modest: "The campaign, labeled 'Take Back Yoga', does not ask yoga devotees to become Hindu, or instructors to teach more about Hinduism. The small but increasingly influential group behind it, the Hindu American Foundation, suggests only that people become more aware of yoga's debt to the faith's ancient traditions."[5] Sounds innocuous enough, but it prompted a firestorm in response.

---

3. QR code URL: http://www.huffingtonpost.com/2010/10/07/albert-mohler-southern-ba_n_753797.html.
4. QR code URL: http://www.hafsite.org/media/pr/takeyogaback.
5. Paul Vitello, "Hindu Group Stirs a Debate Over Yoga's Soul," New York *Times*, November 27, 2010, http://www.nytimes.com/2010/11/28/nyregion/28yoga.html?src=me&ref=homepage&_r=0.

Check out this short informative video from the Hindu Student Association.[6]

Perhaps most notably, it led to what has become known as the Shukla-Chopra great yoga debate—a debate about the "Hindu-ness" of yoga. Aseem Shukla, co-founder and board member of the HAF, wrote an essay on Hinduism and yoga, arguing that yoga is deeply rooted in Hinduism, and separating them does violence both to the integrity of yoga itself and also (and especially) to the Hindu community in the United States. He writes:

 Find the text of the debate here.[7]

> Why is yoga severed in America's collective consciousness from Hinduism? Yoga, meditation, ayurvedic natural healing, self-realization—they are today's syntax for New Age, Eastern, mystical, even Buddhist, but nary an appreciation of their Hindu origins. It is not surprising, then, that Hindu schoolchildren complain that Hinduism is conflated only with caste, cows, exoticism and polytheism—the salutary contributions and philosophical underpinnings lost and ignored. The severance of yoga from Hinduism disenfranchises millions of Hindu Americans from their spiritual heritage and a legacy in which they can take pride.[8]

Here's how he ends his piece, and I quote him at length:

> All of this is not to contend, of course, that yoga is only for Hindus. Yoga is Hinduism's gift to humanity to follow, practice and experience. No one can ever be asked to leave their own religion or reject their own theologies or to convert to a pluralistic tradition such as Hinduism. Yoga asks only that one follow the path of yoga for it will necessarily lead one to become a better Hindu, Christian, Jew or Muslim. Yoga, like its Hindu origins, does not offer ways to believe in God; it offer [*sic*] ways to know God.
>   But be forewarned. Yogis say that the dedicated practice of yoga will subdue the restless mind, lessen one's cravings for the mundane material

---

6. QR code URL: http://www.youtube.com/watch?v=gNcx8H7pcMg&feature=channel_video_title.
7. QR code URL: http://www.faithstreet.com/onfaith/2010/04/30/shukla-and-chopra-the-great-yoga-debate/4379.
8. http://www.faithstreet.com/onfaith/2010/04/30/shukla-and-chopra-the-great-yoga-debate/4379.

world and put one on the path of self-realization—that each individual is a spark of the Divine. Expect conflicts if you are sold on the exclusivist claims of Abrahamic faiths—that their God awaits the arrival of only His chosen few at heaven's gate—since yoga shows its own path to spiritual nlightenment to all seekers regardless of affiliation.

Hindus must take back yoga and reclaim the intellectual property of their spiritual heritage—not sell out for the expediency of winning more clients for the yoga studio down the street.[9]

What was Deepak Chopra's response? "Sorry, your patent on yoga has run out." Basically, Chopra, a prominent Indian American physician who incorporates Hindu traditional medicine into his practice, argues what others have argued: yoga's origins in India predate the existence of what we now call "Hinduism," and therefore it is a spiritual (not religious) practice open and available to all. Additionally, there are others who would agree that yoga has Hindu roots, but would say that Christians can not only practice yoga, but in doing so, they can strengthen their own faith. An example of this is John Sheveland, professor at Gonzaga University, who writes, "Surely a physical practice that respects both body and mind merits the attention of Christians seeking greater respect and stewardship of the bodies of creation."[10] And there is even a Website dedicated to "Christians practicing yoga," whose subheading is a quote taken from 1 Corinthians: "Do you not know that your body is a temple of the Holy Spirit within you which you have from God? . . . Therefore, glorify God in your body" (1 Cor. 6:19, 20). The Website has many different resources that offer both information and practical advice.

 See the Christians Practicing Yoga Website here.[11]

The debate on both sides of the issues raises important questions for both Christians and Christian educators. For example, what am I, a seminary professor, supposed to say to a student who has begun practicing yoga in earnest, especially if I know her candidacy committee (or other judicatory body) might have some concerns about that? Is a college or university chapel a good space for a more "Hindu-leaning" yoga class? Why or why not?

As I said before, there are no simple answers to these questions. I have laid all this out not to persuade anyone one way or the other but, rather, to make the case for being informed, and to emphasize that the popularity of yoga in the United States offers a wonderful opportunity (some might even say the necessity) for learning more about just what Hinduism is, exactly, and how the tenets of yoga are

---

9. Ibid.
10. John N. Sheveland, "Is Yoga Religious?," *Christian Century* (June 14, 2011), 23.
11. QR code URL: http://www.christianspracticingyoga.com.

related to it. Here's an example: the word *yoga* itself has a very interesting history and usage in Hinduism.

The Sanskrit verb from which the word is taken means "to yoke" or "to join." Originally, the verb simply referred to the harnessing of oxen to a plow or horses to a cart. Over time, however, it developed an explicitly religious use, specifically pointing to the means by which one facilitated a connection with the divine: in that context, it refers to "joining," "attaching," or "uniting." For example, the *Bhagavad-Gita* (one of the most important and popular sacred texts of Hinduism) teaches four different "yogas"—paths or disciplines—by which an individual can attain liberation: the way of wisdom, *jñana-yoga;* the way of mental focus and concentration, *raja-yoga;* the way of devotional love, *bhakti-yoga;* and the way of dedicated and intentional service in action in the world, *karma-yoga.*[12] These different paths were described and taught in a variety of Hindu philosophical and religious contexts long before the *Gita* was written, and all of them continue to play an important role in the religious lives of Hindus, even though every individual does not emphasize and practice each of the disciplines equally. Turning back to Christianity, then, it would seem natural that Christians who are interested in yoga might do well to ask about their own "connection" with God, and particularly how the body participates in that—if it does at all. I'd like to conclude this section with some reflections on that idea.

Thinking about the Body

Let's return to Mohler's comment about the body. Regardless of what you think about yoga, I find his statement rejecting the idea that "the body is a vehicle for reaching consciousness with the divine" very incongruous coming from a Christian, since the core, defining claim of Christianity is that God took on a real human body in the person of Jesus of Nazareth, becoming fully human in order to redeem, reconcile, and restore our full humanity, including our bodies. After all, Jesus himself was resurrected in the body—as evidenced by the scars on his hands and on his side, which he invited Thomas to touch, and his eating of a piece of broiled fish in the presence of his disciples. After all, Christians themselves are supposed to really mean it when they confess a belief in "the resurrection of the body." This language is not simply a metaphor for something purely spiritual, it's a very concrete affirmation that all of who we are will be taken up and transformed in the kingdom of God. What's more, in baptism—the rite of initiation for Christians—Christians are united in their own bodies to the body of Jesus Christ: either that means something literally and physically, or it doesn't mean anything at all.

And this isn't all. Coming out of the Lutheran tradition, with its strong sacramental emphasis on the real presence in the Eucharist, I find it not only incongruous but even absurd and bizarre to deny the body a role in our relationship with God. Of course, "the body" is a vehicle for realizing the divine: in the Lutheran

---

12. John Moffitt, "The Bhagavad Gita as a Way-Shower to the Transcendental," *Theological Studies* 38, no. 2 (June 1977): 317.

church, we profess that very thing every Sunday when we celebrate the Eucharist. In the Lord's Supper, we receive Jesus Christ himself in the flesh—his body and blood in, with, and under the elements of bread and wine. We eat his body and drink his blood, and in so doing, the gathered community together becomes the physical body of Christ, bearing Christ in our physical bodies.

This whole idea of excluding the body from communion with God so clearly demonstrates why the Christian church as a whole seems to have such a difficult time talking about the body in general, and sex in particular (that's a topic for another time). Most of the time, Christians don't talk about the body at all, unless and until there is a problem: a problem with sex, a problem with obesity, a problem with an eating disorder, a problem with disease or illness. Most of us, it seems, have no idea how to talk about the quotidian role the body plays in our relationship with God: taking walks in the woods, holding hands with a partner, enjoying an ice cream cone, swimming in the ocean, warming one's feet in front of a fire, making love, and yes, even practicing yoga. How are these prayer practices? How are these moments for experiencing the divine? How do these activities praise and celebrate God?

Again, then: regardless of what you think about yoga, it seems to me that interreligious conversations in particular around yoga afford the welcome opportunity to give more thought to what it means for Christians, concretely and specifically, that we use our bodies as a means of communicating the presence of the divine to others, and that we ourselves experience a revelation of God in and through the bodies of others. Learning more about Hinduism—and having conversation with Hindus—would offer a helpful contribution to these important reflections.

Praxis Point #3

The question of whether Christians can and should do yoga—and in what "spirit" they should if they choose to (that is, as a spiritual discipline/ritual practice or as mere exercise)—is, indeed, something that is worth considering, but it is not necessarily an issue that makes or breaks quality interreligious engagement with the Hindu community. While some individuals become quite animated over this debate, for many Hindus this is a nonissue, and it is entirely possible to build interreligious relationships in the Hindu community in which the question of yoga never emerges. If one takes a tour of a Hindu temple, for example, one is unlikely to see people practicing poses such as "downward-facing dog" and "pigeon" inside. What, then, can readers take from this conversation that can practically inform their relationships with Hindus? For one thing, greater awareness of the issues can translate into greater sensitivities to those places in which one might unintentionally cause offense. Additionally, and as mentioned previously, such an awareness around those places where Christians experience "holy envy" can lead to meaningful conversations about appropriate and inappropriate ways to incorporate similar aspects into one's Christian practice. Such holy envy can also lead individuals to dig more deeply into their own Christian traditions to find those places where similar practices or rituals might exist. There may not be an equivalent ancient physical ritual practice in Christianity, but such holy envy could lead to a greater appreciation of other forms of Christian embodied prayer such as liturgical dance.

Additionally, an awareness of the issues behind something as seemingly innocuous as a yoga practice can heighten one's sensitivity to the myriad ways in which the religious symbols, iconography, and practice of other traditions can be misappropriated and, potentially, watered down in our secular society. Take, for example, a tiny little thing such as the two-letter word "*Om*"[13] that is often chanted during yoga classes and printed on t-shirts and yoga pants. (It is also a rather popular tattoo.) For many Hindus, the chanting of "Om" is a sacred act. It represents the absolute, Brahman. It encapsulates the most dramatic and profound concepts of the universe in one tiny syllable. Prayers begin and end with this sacred sound which is often followed by "Shanti" or "peace." According to the sacred texts, the past, present, and future are wrapped up in this word, and those who know this syllable and chant it rightly are connected to the wisdom and mystery of the universe; the vibrations connect individuals across time and space. For Christians, chanting "Om" is tantamount to reciting the creeds or the ancient "Jesus Prayer" of the Orthodox Church. It is a verbal sacrament. Given its place in the tradition, one has to wonder, then, whether it is appropriate to chant the "Om" while sitting, sweaty and cross-legged in lotus position, at the end of a gym-based yoga practice. If placed within its proper context, there might, indeed, be a benefit to ending a yoga class with "Om," but if not contextualized as a sacred chant, then the repetition of "Om" can ring hollow and, potentially, cause offense.

This, however, is probably not the first question that those who visit a Hindu temple or interact with Hindu neighbors will have to entertain. On a visit to a temple or even a family's personal altar at home, there are other traditions and practices that could, potentially, be equally as concerning that non-Hindus must consider. These issues relate to how one interacts in a non-Christian setting as a guest and outside observer.

Before taking a group to visit a non-Christian setting, it is incumbent on the group leader to prepare participants fully for what to expect. This can vary from the sacred to the profane. What attire is appropriate? What about a head covering for women? Are pants or skirts appropriate? Should shoulders and knees be covered? Will shoes be kept on or removed? (Hole-y socks or unmanicured toes, after all, can be an embarrassment!) Should visitors be prepared to sit on the floor? Can they take notes? (Often, in Orthodox Jewish settings this is verboten on the Sabbath.) Are cell phones allowed? And when the group gets inside, what should it expect? Do men and women sit together? Will there be a formal "program"? In what language will prayers or a service be

---

13. QR code URL: http://www.breakoutofthebox.com/Om.htm.

conducted? Will visitors be expected to go through the same physical motions as members of the community?

These are all important questions. Answering them in advance of a visit can help to build the confidence of participants and prepare them for what to expect. Anticipating questions such as these prior to a visit can make the difference in the quality of experience that participants have. There are some excellent resources to help prepare visitors, including the *How to Be a Perfect Stranger*[14] series and *Do I Kneel or Do I Bow?*[15]

For visits to communities in the Hindu and Sikh traditions, it is also worth preparing participants for the offering of *prasadam*. *Prasadam* is literally translated as "the Lord's" or "Krishna's mercy." In the Hindu context, it is food that has been offered to the gods. At the end of many Hindu and Sikh services, *prasadam* is offered to the congregants as a means of offering the blessings of the deity to those gathered. The *prasad* (sometimes a sweet, warm, gooey confection made from butter, sugar, and flour) is distributed throughout the congregation to any and all who will take it. For some Christians, this can become problematic. First Corinthians 8 offers clear directives about eating food offered to idols. Some visitors to a Hindu temple might be concerned about taking the *prasadam* based on this passage, but they might be concerned about not taking the *prasadam* based on etiquette.

As we reflect on the embodied aspect of prayer, the question of etiquette and participation is particularly salient for invitations to worship in the Muslim context. Many Christians find the Muslim *rakats*, or postures of prayer, to be especially meaningful and symbolic—even more so than Hindu yoga practices, which are meant to provide comfort in prolonged meditative states. The act of prostrating oneself during Muslim prayer—of literally placing one's head on the floor—is quite humbling. It is the physical embodiment of the concept of submission that is at the heart of the Islamic self-understanding. Many first-time visitors to a mosque find this to be an overwhelming, moving, and emotional aspect of Muslim worship. At the same time, many others are quite uncomfortable with the prospect of participating in Muslim prayer postures. It feels to some as if they are bowing down to other gods.

Situations such as these need to be discussed in advance of a visit in order to make everyone as comfortable as possible and in order to anticipate concerns and needs appropriately. In almost all situations, it is perfectly acceptable for visitors to a new religious setting to be present as participant-observers. In this understanding, all visitors are welcome to watch, observe, and participate as they are comfortable. For some, this might mean hanging in the back and soaking up all of the new sights, sounds, and smells. For others, it might mean

14. Stuart M. Matlins and Arthur J. Magida, eds., *How to Be a Perfect Stranger: The Essential Religious Etiquette Handbook*, 5th ed. (Woodstock, VT: Skylight Paths, 2010), http://www.skylightpaths.com /page/product/978-1-59473-294-2.

15. Akasha Lonsdale, *Do I Kneel or Do I Bow? What You Need to Know When Attending Religious Occasions* (New York: Random House, 2010), http://www.randomhouse.com/book/103499 /do-i-kneel-or-do-i-bow-by-akasha-lonsdale.

jumping in fully and embodying all of the motions and rituals—the sounds, tastes, and smells—of a tradition. Both can be appropriate and accommodated in group or individual visits.—*Christy Lohr Sapp*

Burning a Qur'an?

Perhaps you remember the fuss that was generated by the Florida pastor, Terry Jones, who has made an (infamous) name for himself as the "Qur'an-burning pastor." An NPR story from September 2013 notes that Jones was actually arrested that year before he had the chance to burn 2,998 Qur'ans on the anniversary of 9/11.[16] And 2013 wasn't even his first time: back in 2010, Jones made international news when both President Obama and Defense Secretary Robert Gates publically asked Jones to rethink his proposed Qur'an burning that year—Gates even called Jones personally. Jones relented, but then changed his mind and, in March 2011, went ahead and supervised the burning: "Yesterday, during Dove World Outreach Center's Sunday service, without any publicity and under the supervision of Jones, Pastor Wayne Sapp soaked

Dala'il al-Khayrat Qu'ran (Chester Beatty Library, 2010). Public domain.

a Quran in kerosene for an hour, held an event he said was a 'trial' for the Muslim holy book, and after the book was found guilty, Sapp set the Quran on fire using a barbecue lighter."[17] Finally, he also burned a Qur'an in 2012, as a way to protest the imprisonment of Youcef Nadarkhani, an Iranian Christian pastor.[18] Although the attending audience was small, the event was streamed live over the Internet, and can be found on YouTube. After each of these events, there were riots overseas that ended in death.

Now, I'd like to think that most Christians would agree that it is wrong to burn a Qur'an, but it also matters to me that Christians in particular come to that conclusion for religious, not simply pragmatic, reasons. In my read of their responses, President Obama and Robert Gates weren't concerned about the religious rationale for arguing against such an action but, rather, because they feared American soldiers deployed overseas would experience retaliatory consequences. That

---

16. http://www.npr.org/blogs/thetwo-way/2013/09/11/221528510/pastor-terry-jones-arrested-before-planned-quran-burning.
17. http://www.npr.org/blogs/thetwo-way/2011/03/21/134743260/controversial-florida-pastor-reneges-and-supervises-burning-of-quran.
18. http://www.theblaze.com/stories/2012/04/29/pastor-terry-jones-burns-koran-to-protest-iranian-pastors-imprisonment/.

is certainly important, of course, but here I'd like to think theologically and ask why Christians—specifically Christian ministry professionals—might argue against burning a Qur'an, particularly once they have a better understanding of how the Qur'an functions in Islam.

Of course, as Christians we can make a strong argument simply from Jesus' call to love the neighbor, and Paul's exhortation not to put a stumbling block before others: Why in the world would we engage in an activity that is so deeply painful and offensive to other people of faith? Such actions should be ruled entirely out of bounds by anyone claiming to be a disciple of Jesus Christ. However, there is more here than most Christians even know, and that is because the Qur'an does not have the same role in Islam that the Bible has in Christianity: even though many Christians would be outraged if they were to hear about Bibles being burned by Muslims, the latter action actually pales in comparison to the former. In the rest of this section, I'd like to explain why, and offer some important information that can help Christian students, in particular Christian seminarians, think more sensitively about what the Qur'an is, and why Christians in particular should stand and speak out against anyone who would burn one.

Praxis Point #4

This issue speaks of one of the most popular ways to engage across interreligious lines—through joint acts of service, advocacy, and activism. In being good neighbors, we are often called on to be advocates for change and partners in solidarity. We are also called, at times, to work across religious difference for the greater good. In so doing, we can learn much about ourselves, our own traditions, and others' traditions as well.

On the university campus where I serve, there is a "bias response team" that is called on to deal with student conduct involving discriminatory acts or demonstrations of religious, sexual, racial, and other kinds of bias. Several years ago, the Jewish students created a holy uproar when they awoke to find swastikas painted on various walls around campus. These did not seem to be targeting specific Jewish students, as they were not painted on any individual's dorm rooms or on the Center for Jewish Life, but were painted on a bridge and benches that are often covered over with student messages. Still, the Jewish and LGBT communities responded with outrage because of the negative associations of the swastika with Nazi propaganda and discriminatory bullying. As a result, the use of swastikas was officially equated with "hate speech" by the university administrators.

 The Hindu community, however, had a dramatically different reaction to the situation. For them, the swastika is a symbol of good luck, well-being, and prosperity. The ancient symbol[19] actually has resonance with a number of religious communities,

---

19. QR Code URL: http://timesofindia.indiatimes.com/city/bangalore-times/What-the-Swastika-means /articleshow/994390.cms.

including Hindus, Buddhists, Jains, and early Christians. Hindu students were hurt that a symbol that they value and prize was immediately dismissed as hateful by the larger community. This prompted interesting conversations on campus. Faculty in the Jewish community were reluctant to turn those conversations into an open interreligious dialogue about symbol, meaning, and the use of the swastika, but the event and the advocacy in response to it were a telling example of the ways in which communities can come together in advocacy around acts of aggression and violence.

Interfaith service can take many different forms, and the interfaith-service movement is sweeping college and university campuses thanks, in part, to President Obama and his 2010 Interfaith and Community Service Campus Challenge.[20] This initiative called on colleges and universities to integrate interreligious engagement into their community-service activities in order to create greater reflection on a shared ethic of responsibility to neighbors across belief systems. The basic premise is that, at the end of the day, all people can agree and work together on certain aspects of community improvement regardless of belief and practice. The challenge grows from the growing recognition of service as a common meeting point. Christians, Muslims, Jews, and Buddhists might not agree on what happens after death or whether there is a place called "heaven," but they can all swing a hammer to help build a house for a homeless family or package meals for the hungry.

Interreligious service opens the door for conversations on myriad topics and touch points while also moving participants out of their "heads" and into their "hands." It can also be smartly tailored to reflect the issues of the wider world or to the particular needs of a community. Don't have an issue with Qur'an burning in your town? That's OK. Perhaps you have a river that needs cleaning up or a chemical company that is menacing low-income communities. Most of our religious traditions have something to say about creation care, and a follow-up reflection to the hard work of tree planting or garden building can revolve around what different traditions say about stewardship of the earth and healing the world (*tikkun olam*). Maybe your community has a large population of refugees or immigrants that can foster projects and conversations around hospitality, exodus, or migration. Maybe work with non-Christians in the local prison can raise awareness of captivity and release in different traditions. In North Carolina, an interreligious movement has grown in the past two years from faith-inspired leaders coming together at the state capitol to speak out against harmful legislative decisions around immigration, voter rights, and education cuts. Moral Mondays[21] have drawn support from pastors, rabbis, and imams as well as social-justice advocates from every race, vocation, and socioeconomic

---

20. QR code URL: http://www.whitehouse.gov/administration/eop/ofbnp/interfaithservice.
21. QR code URL: http://www.motherjones.com/politics/2014/04/william-barber-moral-monday-north-carolina.

background. It is a great example of interreligious voices uniting around issues of concern for local communities.

In planning interreligious service projects, it is important to keep a number of things in mind, and there is a growing online collection of resource material on planning such opportunities. One good place to go for resourcing is the InterFaith Youth Core (IFYC).[22] As a prime agent in President Obama's campus challenge, the IFYC Website offers toolkits, discussion guides, syllabi, case studies, and "transferrable tips" for interreligious engagement. There is even a video, "4 Ways to Make a Service Project Interfaith."[23] Interreligious service projects work best when they are jointly planned and owned by a mixed constituency. This allows everyone involved to have "buy-in" around the service goal. Connecting that goal to some shared theme is also helpful. Initiatives fail to be interreligious when only one group does all of the planning, agenda setting, decision making, and outcome building. Projects should be marked by a clear sense of service that is separate from any sense of evangelization. Postservice reflection is a perfect place to discuss the various motivations for service—some of which might include a response to God's call in one's life—but the service itself is best kept free from anything that could be construed as coercion toward belief.

National days of community service can be a great place to start in identifying a theme or prompt for interreligious service. Martin Luther King Day and 9/11 are now both national days of service in which communities are encouraged to get out and work together for the greater good. The United Nations has also identified a number of international observances[24] that can serve as good prompts for interreligious initiatives. The International Day of Social Justice, for example, might inspire a conversation about human rights and homelessness. International Women's Day might prompt work at a women's shelter or crisis clinic and lead to conversations about gender roles in different traditions.

Positive interreligious responses to negative events such as Qur'an burning and human trafficking can do double duty toward educating individuals about justice issues in their own traditions while also providing an opportunity to learn more about and learn to advocate for another's tradition.—*Christy Lohr Sapp*

What Is the Qur'an?

Imagine, if you will, that one morning you read a story about a group of atheists who had gotten together to burn a pile of Bibles. How would you feel? For myself, I think I would be disgusted and angry—I don't like book burning in any

---

22. QR code URL: http://www.ifyc.org/.
23. QR code URL: http://ifyc.org/resources/4-ways-make-service-project-interfaith.
24. QR code URL: http://www.un.org/en/events/observances/days.shtml.

form, frankly—and I would recognize it as a symbolic attack on Christianity, as I'm sure it would have been intended. However, I would not consider the burning of a Bible a *literal* attack on my faith: what I mean by that is that, for me (and for Christianity in general, I would say), the Bible itself—that is, the paper and ink of the physical book—is not considered sacred. Its holiness comes from Christ (the superlative "Word" of God), to whom it bears witness, not the pages on which the words appear. That is, the Bible is holy because it is the "cradle of Christ" (to use Martin Luther's phrase), not because it in and of itself is divine. I don't "believe in" the Bible—I believe in God, whose loving relationship with humanity and all of creation lies at the heart of the biblical narrative.

Another way of thinking about this is to think about how you treat your own Bible at home. One could make a persuasive argument that the sign of a Bible being treated "properly" is that it is beat up and marked up, with a bent spine and turned-down pages. That is, a Bible is meant to be *used*—not kept under glass and venerated like an idol. So, if you spill a little coffee on it or rip a page—no big deal: you haven't harmed anything of God's being or nature in your carelessness. The Bible may be inspired by God, but the words themselves were not spoken into the ear of the writers of the different books—and we have many different early manuscripts of the Bible, not all of which agree (which is why we have a "shorter" and a "longer" ending of the Gospel of Mark, for example). Thus, the words themselves are not the literal "word of God"—Jesus Christ is the only literal "Word of God" in Christianity, and it is in him that my faith ultimately abides, not in a book—even a book that tells his story. For Muslims, however, it is quite different.

The Nuts and Bolts of the Qur'an

The Qur'an (you sometimes still see the older spelling "Koran," but in fact, "Qur'an" is a more accurate transliteration of the Arabic) is roughly the size of the New Testament: it has 114 chapters (called *surahs*), which contain around 6,300 verses (called *ayas*).[25] Like the Bible, you typically see passages referred to by chapter and verse; unlike the Bible, however, the Qur'an is not written in a narrative form, in a chronological order. Instead, there are discrete chapters on a variety of topics, some of which repeat important information also emphasized in other chapters. Each chapter has a different title and, typically, that title is a word found in the chapter itself—maybe a name of a character or a topical theme. Every single chapter (save one) begins with a phrase that is known as the *basmala*: "In the name of God, the merciful one, the compassionate one."

So far, so good—but now let's get to the heart of it. While most Christians believe that the Bible is "inspired" by God, the way in which that actual inspiration happens is typically understood to be more general, more abstract, and less literal and concrete. So, Christians might think about the Holy Spirit moving the hearts of

---

25. A good place to start reading about the Qur'an is John Kaltner's *Introducing the Qur'an for Today's Reader* (Minneapolis: Fortress Press, 2011).

the individuals who wrote the different books, but not actually moving their pens across the parchment. Or, Christians might envision the Holy Spirit suggesting ideas and images in their minds, but not actually putting words into their mouths, as it were. For Muslims, it is just the opposite.

For Muslims, the Qur'an stands as the definitive, exact word of God (*Allah*), which was spoken directly to the prophet Muhammad by the angel Gabriel. Thus, when reading the Qur'an, Muslims believe that the Arabic text is quite literally the voice, the speech of God. And indeed, while there were debates early in the tradition about the nature of the Qur'an (was it created or uncreated?), since the end of the tenth century, the mainstream Muslim community has regarded the Qur'an as the literal and uncreated Word of God—the image of the eternal "word" that resides with God in heaven.

The word *qur'an* actually means to "read" or "recite." It is said that Muhammad received his first communication from Gabriel one night in the year 610 CE, when a voice from heaven called out to Muhammad with the command to "recite," and from that point on, for roughly the next twenty years, Muhammad received direct revelations from God, which he then memorized and shared with others. During his lifetime, then, the Qur'an was a living, dynamic "text" whose surahs Muhammad would order and reorder, following Gabriel's guidance. The Qur'an remained an oral text until the caliphate of Uthman, who ordered scholars to create a definitive version of the text, which was established in 650. Still today, most Muslims consider the Uthmanic "recension" to be the perfect record of the exact words that God spoke to Muhammad through Gabriel, with no errors or alterations.

So, to be clear, the Qur'an is actually much more like Jesus than it is like the Bible, in terms of how it functions in the religion itself. In the same way that Christians believe that Jesus is God's perfect Word and God's definitive revelation, Muslims believe the same thing about the Qur'an (so, interestingly enough, both traditions actually are grounded on a "word" of God). That is, Muslims believe that the Qur'an is a flawless, incomparable, inerrant revelation of God's will that cannot ever be surpassed or superseded. This also explains why translations of the Qur'an are so problematic. Translations into vernacular languages are allowed, but it is clear that they do not hold the same weight and authority as the Arabic. Simply put, God spoke to Muhammad in Arabic; therefore, any translation is a "loss" of meaning, and a step away from God, as it were. This is why the five daily prayers are done in Arabic, and why memorization of the Arabic is strongly encouraged, even if one doesn't know the language. The words themselves have power—the text is meant to be recited and heard, not simply read quietly to oneself—and it is believed that when the Qur'an is recited aloud one is brought into the presence of God.

Regarding the message of the Qur'an, it is pretty straightforward, even if the chapters are not organized in a way that is obvious to Christians when reading it for the first time. Muslims believe that God sent messengers over and over to God's people throughout history, culminating with the sending of Muhammad to Arabia, and entrusting him with the same message and the same mission God had given to the earlier prophets: to call humanity back to the right way of life, to communicate God's true guidance afresh and to organize into one community all who responded to his teaching. The Qur'an is the book that embodies this mission and guidance, as revealed by God to Muhammad; and it is why there will be no more prophets. Humanity no longer needs a prophet, an interpreter of God's will and God's word, because we have the definitive, unsurpassable example of God's word in the Qur'an.

The Qur'an teaches several key doctrines. First, that God created the whole world and is the sovereign ruler of the whole world. God created humanity, of course, and endowed humans with intelligence, reason, and the ability to know good and evil and to act rightly. Life in this world is not permanent, and in many ways it is to be seen as a testing ground for the life to come: at our death we will return to God and be judged on the basis of how we acted on earth and either rewarded eternally in paradise or punished eternally in hell. To be Muslim means to "submit" to God (the root of both "Muslim" and "Islam") and therefore obedience to God's will is of central importance—and the source of knowledge of God's will, first and foremost, is the Qur'an.

So, perhaps, then, it should be obvious why burning a Qur'an is not the same thing as burning a Bible—the parallel would be to burning Jesus, and—to our shame—we all know how that worked out for the Jews through the centuries: the Jews were persecuted for centuries throughout Europe in no small part because they were blamed in the Christian tradition for Jesus' crucifixion. For Muslims, the book itself is sacred, and it is always treated with care and respect; one should always be clean and purified when one holds and reads the Qur'an, and it should always be stored carefully. What's more, in a manner similar to Orthodox Jews, pious Muslims believe that once a Qur'an becomes too worn out or damaged to use, it shouldn't simply be thrown away but, rather, must be properly disposed, in a way that it fitting to the holiness of the words. The favored way of doing this is wrapping the Qur'an and burying it deeply in the ground. It can also be stored in a safe place; and caches of "paper graves" have been found in the Middle East dating from the seventh century. These disposal practices, of course, are not necessary for translations, only for the Qur'an written in Arabic. However, even translations should be treated with respect.

For me, this is one of the best examples of why interreligious understanding is so important in our world today. Without a clear knowledge of what the Qur'an is and how it functions for Muslims, Christians are ill-prepared to formulate an opinion or offer a response when others raise questions about the Qur'an in general, or this specific case in particular. (One is reminded here, too, of the reported cases from Guantanamo Bay detention center where the Qur'an was intentionally desecrated to torment the Muslim prisoners there). For Christians, it's not enough to condemn these acts for the physical and psychic harm they cause; it is also necessary to speak out as fellow believers against what is so clearly a religious violation, which compromises the credibility of us all.

Can/Should Christians Practice Buddhist Meditation?

Have you ever meditated? If you are like most people, and think of the word in its most general sense, the answer is probably yes—even if to you, "meditate" signifies little more than sitting quietly and reflecting and/or relaxing. When most Christians think of meditation, this is usually what they have in mind—sitting quietly, and maybe thinking about a Scripture passage, or repeating a simple prayer: "Lord, have mercy."

Photo: Eric Pouhier. CC-by-SA 2.5 Generic license (Wikimedia Commons).

Some Christians, however, dabble in Buddhist meditation—or even practice it in a much more formal way. The most common place to experience this, typically, is at a Unitarian Universalist Church, many of which host weekly or biweekly Buddhist communities. For example, in Gettysburg, Pennsylvania, the Unitarian Universalist community hosts a "Buddhist Insight Meditation Group" (from the Theravada tradition) every Sunday night. [26]

From both reading and personal experience, the appeal of Buddhist meditation is twofold. First, it offers a positive experience not typically afforded in most Christian services. In the majority of mainline Protestant, Catholic, and evangelical services, there is very little quiet time. In my experience of the Lutheran church, for example, if, on a Sunday morning, the pastor waits too long between any parts of the liturgy, everyone immediately becomes uncomfortable and assumes something is wrong. Even more, the experience of silence and quiet mindfulness is something our contemporary culture encourages us to avoid actively. My ever-present cell phone entices me at every moment, with *The New York Times* app, the latest book on download, Netflix, YouTube, and so forth—and that's only if I have no one to call, text, or Skype at the moment. I have no reason to be by myself, to be silent, *ever*. Many of us, however, realize the inevitable costs that come with such busyness, such mental, visual, and audial clutter, such perpetual distraction: more stress, more anxiety, less peace.

In such a climate, the appeal of intentional meditation practices seems obvious; and, for Christians, there is the added advantage that many American Buddhist teachers—and certainly many popular writers in the genre of Christian spirituality—emphasize that one need not compromise any aspect of one's Christian belief to practice meditation. Often, Buddhist teachers who specifically focus on nonimmigrant American populations stress the nontheistic aspect of Buddhism, and even encourage Christians to continue to go to church while they are engaging in specific meditation practices.

This is, in no small part, why the phenomenon of "double-religious belonging," which is becoming more common in the United States, typically occurs with

---

26. http://www.uugettysburg.org/.

Christianity and Buddhism, where an individual self-identifies as a Buddhist-Christian, for example. Perhaps the best-known example is Paul Knitter, prolific scholar of interreligious dialogue, who describes himself as a "Buddhist Christian" rather than a "Christian Buddhist"—it does make a difference which word is the adjective and which is the noun. He even has written a book about it: *Without Buddha I Could Not Be a Christian*, where he writes, "Buddhism has enabled me to make sense of my Christian faith so that I can maintain my intellectual integrity and affirm what I see as true and good in my culture; but at the same time,

it has aided me to carry out my prophetic-religious responsibility and challenge what I see as false and harmful in my culture."[27] He acknowledges that some may see this as "spiritual sleeping around,"[28] but insists that his practice of Buddhism actually has deepened and strengthened his appreciation and understanding of the Christian faith.

It seems clear to me that there are several specific characteristics of Buddhism that make it appealing—and nonthreatening—to Christians. For example, unlike Christianity (and Judaism and Islam, for that matter), there is no demand for exclusive adherence; nor is there a competing deity that demands worship. Thus, the specific practices of Buddhism, such as meditation, can be much more easily adopted into a Christian framework as little more than a means to a (Christian) end, or techniques for self- or spiritual development. When we look more closely at what meditation is and how it functions in a Buddhist context, however, a more complex and problematic picture is revealed.

Buddhist monk meditating in Ramkhamhaeng National Park, Thailand. Photo: Tevaprapas Makklay. CCA 3.0 Unported license (Wikimedia Commons).

What Is Buddhist Meditation?[29]

Paul Griffiths notes that "meditational practice has always been of central importance to Buddhist soteriology and Buddhist philosophical theory."[30] At the same time, however, it is important to recognize that in today's context, "meditation"

27. Paul F. Knitter, *Without Buddha I Could Not Be a Christian* (Oxford, UK: Oneworld, 2009), xii.
28. Ibid., 213.
29. This information is taken from my book, *Rethinking Salvation: What Christians Can Learn from Buddhism* (Minneapolis: Fortress Press, 2009).
30. Paul J. Griffiths, "Indian Buddhist Meditation," in *Buddhist Spirituality*, ed. Takeuchi Yoshinori (New York: Crossroad, 1993), 34.

is a deceptive term, because while it suggests something very simple and easy to explain, in actuality, when it comes to Buddhist meditation in particular, it has both varied and detailed descriptions that belie easy generalizations.

Buddhism as a whole contains a vast of number of texts that describe the practice of meditation with great philosophical sophistication and extreme complexity. In fact, there is an expression, frequently encountered in Buddhist literature, of "84,000 dharma doors," which points to the manifold ways of entering into the experience of enlightenment. Suffice it to say, then, that a full analysis and description of meditation in Buddhism lies far outside the scope of a book such as this—in fact, such would be more confusing that clarifying. So, in lieu of that, let me offer just a few different aspects of meditation by means of introduction.

The "How" of Meditation: Concentration, Contemplation, and Visualization

There are three aspects of meditation that often are mentioned in descriptions of Buddhist meditation: *concentration*, *contemplation*, and *visualization*. They can go together, but they are not the same; however, each contributes to experience of enlightenment in its own way. First, concentration practices guide the meditator to focus attention on one specific aspect of their immediate experience, such as the Zen practice of focusing attention on the breath. Other objects of concentration are frequently encountered in the literature, including visual objects (a blue circle, for example), and auditory objects (a repeated word or phrase, which will be discussed more fully below under the category "mantra"). Second, contemplation practices often are seen as a second stage of the developing meditative practitioner's skill; having learned to focus the attention on some specific, immediately present sensory object, the mind is now "relaxed" and attention is opened to a wider range of the experienced whole of the present moment.

Third, visualization practices engage the practitioner in the development of an internal mental "world," usually accessed through an active process of creating an inner visual image. Some such practices are relatively simple—for example, concentrating on a blue circle is followed by forming an inner visual image of that blue circle. Others are very complicated practices in which the practitioner creates an internal image of a Buddhist deity, including all the accompanying iconographic details. This brief summary in no way exhausts the possibilities, but I hope it gives the reader some idea about the variety of meditation practices and their overall importance in the tradition as a whole.

The "Why" of Meditation: Wisdom and Compassion

Meditation has been called "the heartbeat" of Buddhism, and few would dispute that the various practices of meditation are foundational to the Buddhist life. Meditation involves wisdom and compassion, the two central components of the path of enlightenment, and it is a primary means by which one shakes the hold of ignorance, greed, and anger. The goal of meditation is the realization of nirvana—that is, the experience of enlightenment and realization of the true nature of reality—but that in itself does not tell the whole story. Instead, the practice itself, the means, if you will, is also an important component of the goal—the change in one's engagement with the world and one's understanding of reality and oneself. Paul Griffiths writes, "meditation on items of Buddhist doctrine is meant to result . . . not only in knowledge that certain things are true, but also in the alternation of the practitioner's cognitive and perceptual experience to accord with that knowledge."[31] In other words, the practice of meditation results in both intellectual understanding of truth and also the experiential realization of that truth for oneself in one's own life.

Many people are not aware that there is not one single Buddhist description of the definitive, universal form of meditation for all Buddhists in all times and places. Instead, there exists in Buddhism a wide variety of texts that offer a corresponding variety of forms of meditation. So, for example, in Indian Buddhism, we find over forty subjects of meditation, ranging from concentration on simple, concrete objects, in order to develop one's concentration, to visualization of corpses in varying stages of decay, in order to remind the practitioner of the inevitability of death and the impermanence of all life. Different practices are suggested based on one's character and on the particular state of one's religious development. Contrary to popular belief, most Buddhist texts recognize that meditation is a technical skill to be learned, practiced, and developed, akin to learning to play the piano, and for almost no one is the practice natural and innate. Much like the beginning pianist starts by playing scales, so also the novice begins by practicing an awareness of her breath, which is much harder than one might imagine!

It also is important to recognize that many of the texts that discuss meditation emphasize one's physical condition, as well as one's posture, recognizing that the mind and the body do not work independently, and that the state of the latter affects the state of the former, either for good or for ill. So, for example, one work notes the following:

> Now after closing the windows of the senses with the shutters of mindfulness, you should know the proper measure of food that is conducive to meditation and good health. For too much food obstructs the flow of one's breathing, leads to lethargy and sleep, and saps one's strength. And just as too much food produces purposelessness, the consumption of too little food is debilitation. For excessive fasting takes away from the body its substance, its glow, its vitality, its ability to act, and its strength . . . thus, as a practitioner of meditation you should feed our body not out of desire for food or love of it but solely for the purpose of subduing hunger.[32]

This idea of a "middle way" between indulgence and asceticism should be familiar; the Buddha himself adopted such a path before he began the meditation that led him to the realization of nirvana.

---

31. Ibid., 46.
32. From *The Saundarananda of Asvaghosa*, cited in John Strong, *The Experience of Buddhism* (Belmont, CA: Wadsworth, 1995), 121.

Zen Meditation

One of the best-known schools of Buddhism in the West is Zen Buddhism, and it is primarily through Zen that the Buddhist practice of meditation has been brought into the public eye. Therefore, I will give a brief description of meditation as it is practiced in the Zen tradition, in order to give a concrete example of what meditation looks like "in action." Those familiar with Zen may also know the term *zazen*, which refers to a specific type of seated meditation. In this type of meditation, one sits on the floor, on a cushion, in full lotus pose (when possible), with each foot resting on the opposite thigh. The spine is straight, with the left hand resting on top of the right, and the upper body is relaxed but not slumping. For Zen practitioners, this posture is not a means to a different end but, rather, the end itself, as it is believed that when the body is disciplined and properly ordered, the mind will be so as well.

Sojiji Zen Temple's meditation hall, near Tokyo, Japan. Photo: Phokin. CC-by-SA 3.0 Unported license (Wikimedia Commons).

As this posture is being maintained, one is asked to focus on one's breathing—not counting breaths, necessarily, but, rather, saying, "Now I am breathing in one breath," and "Now I am breathing out one breath." As one breathes, one is to feel the breath enter and leave the body, and allow the mind to follow the breath. Instead of trying to fix one's mind on something and hold it there, Zen practitioners are encouraged to observe everything as it happens—be aware of the random thoughts that cross one's mind, be aware of the various discomforts of one's body—but then let them go, not clinging to them, so that thoughts, just like the breath, flow in and out of one's mind naturally. And, that is basically it—but be assured, it is much harder than it looks!

Through this deceptively difficult practice, one experiences one's true nature, which is also called "Buddha-nature," and develops the ability to express this nature not only while in sitting meditation, but also while engaged in the daily activities of one's life. In this way, the practice itself is an end in itself, and not simply the means to something else; and thus meditation itself becomes an experience of nirvana. Since most Christians aren't looking to experience nirvana, nor even experience their "true nature," it's worth asking the question of how these specific, ancient practices of meditation are functioning in a Christian context—and whether or not they are promoting genuine dialogue and interreligious understanding.

Praxis Point #5

The question of meditation is much like the question of yoga. Its prevalence in our society today attempts on many levels to strip the religious history and connotations away from the practice in order to present it as a "sanitized," non-particular exercise in personal betterment and health. And, there are certainly many studies that document the health benefits of meditation. Yet, religious leaders would do well to ask themselves whether presenting meditation in this fashion does a service to the traditions from which it grows. This becomes another issue where it is important to consider the place of "holy envy" along-side potential misappropriation.

A form of meditative prayer or concentration is a component of many of the world religions. For those Christians experiencing holy envy at the mindfulness, discipline, and composure that Buddhist meditation can bring, perhaps investigating those places in Christian tradition that resonate with a similar practice would be appropriate. *Lectio divina* and centering prayer are, admittedly, not entirely the same as guided meditation, but they do provide many of the same benefits in terms of slowing the mind down, focusing on the moment, and deepening awareness of presence and faithfulness.

Christianity has a rich history of practices that includes several examples of meditative-type prayer, and many monasteries and retreat centers offer introductions to these quieter, reflective types of prayer. The Orthodox, Benedictine, and Trappist communities have much to offer the wider Christian world on this topic, and it is no surprise that we have models of dialogue across religious traditions in the lives of those who have made a commitment to regular prayerful reflection in the midst of intentional Christian living. Thomas Merton, for example, provides a great example of East–West dialogue and the integration of Buddhist insights into Christian life. A friend of the Dalai Lama and a meditation leader in his own right, Merton embodies the depth of riches that Christian meditation can offer. My colleagues and I find that students, especially, enjoy the reflection and discipline of meditative prayer, and our spring-break trip to a monastery where cell phones are turned off and the day revolves around chores and prayer is one of our most popular offerings.

Ultimately, focusing on those places in one's own tradition that offer a similar model and objective (for instance, increasing a sense of unity with the presence of God/the divine through silence and contemplation) allows for an in-depth appreciation of one's own tradition while also expanding one's "relatability" to another's. This commitment first to draw from one's own tradition before co-opting practices from another's speaks to the importance of coming to interreligious dialogue from a place of authenticity and rootedness, from what some call a "tradition-constituted" place. The work of Alisdair MacIntyre can inform this thinking for those who want to explore it more deeply. In a nutshell, though, the argument holds that those whose self-identity is formed by a tradition are better dialogue partners because they have a greater sense of who they are and what they believe. Tradition-constituted individuals are governed by the rules, visions, insights, history, and commitments of that tradition. This provides a firm place on which to stand when articulating one's own perspective and in responding to another's. In his book *Whose Justice? Which Rationality?* (Notre Dame, IN: University of Notre Dame Press, 1988), MacIntyre contends that different traditions may develop different responses to similar responses. As far as interreligious dialogue goes, these varied approaches to a common issue provide a basis for sharing, conversation, and mutual enrichment across traditions. When one inhabits her own tradition fully, she is able to recognize the shared concern across differing practices and see how her own tradition attempts to respond to the issue in contradistinction to the other's tradition. Therefore, taking the example of Buddhist meditation, the tradition-constituted Christian can first explore the ways in which Christian history, doctrine, and ritual have supported a contemplative style of prayer and meditation. After discovering this gem in her own tradition, she can then also understand better the benefits, similarities, and differences in Buddhist (or Hindu, Jewish, Muslim, etc.) meditation.—*Christy Lohr Sapp*

"Christian" Seders: Pro or Con?

For my last example, I want to turn to a topic that is fresh in my mind, since I am writing this just a few weeks after Easter: the practice of Christian congregations offering a Seder meal, often in conjunction with a Maundy Thursday service. I have no data to support this, but it seems to me that this practice is occurring more frequently, or maybe in the last decade or so I am just hearing about it more. In any case, I'd like to put the best construal on my neighbor's action and say that the reason more Christians are hosting Seder meals is that they are eager to learn more about Judaism, emphasize Jesus' own Jewish identity, and connect their commemoration of Jesus' final meal with his disciples with the celebration of Passover. I would be remiss, however, if I didn't say that it doesn't always get lived out that way in real life.

A nineteenth-century Ukrainian print depicting a Seder table. Public domain.

The understanding of Jesus' "Last Supper" as a Passover celebration is found in Scripture, of course: particularly in the Gospels of Matthew, Mark, and Luke—John's Gospel says only that it was "before" the festival of the Passover. In the Synoptic Gospels, the writers are explicit that it was a "Passover meal" the disciples prepared, and which they were eating when Jesus instituted what Christians now celebrate as the Lord's Supper. So, perhaps it is logical for Christians to want to recover this original connection and celebrate a "Passover meal" of their own as a part of their Holy Week observances.

In my own experience, this has happened in three different ways. The first option that I have both seen and experienced is when a class, congregation, or individuals are invited to participate in a Seder meal that is hosted by a Jewish community center or synagogue, or that takes place in a private home. Naturally, this is the ideal situation, in that it affords Christians an experience that is the most authentic and provides the most chance for learning and transformation.

The second possibility is where a Christian congregation invites a member of a Jewish community to come and lead them through the Seder meal. Naturally, this also has the potential for learning and growth, particularly to the degree that the congregation lets the Jewish visitor direct and lead both the meal itself as well as the preparations beforehand and the debriefing afterword.

The final possibility, which clearly is the most controversial and fraught with the most potential for disaster is when a Christian congregation chooses to host a Seder meal itself, without any Jewish participation at all. Sometimes these are even referred to as "Christian Seders," which seems to me to only exacerbate the problems. It is this "case" that I would like to explore a bit further. There are many different books, Websites, and other resources that discuss this practice; I want to mention just two—one that is "pro" and one that is "con"—and describe the arguments each makes.

PRO: An Argument for Hosting a "Christian" Seder

In "Introduction to a Christian Seder: Recovering Passover for Christians," Dennis Bratcher of The Church Resource Institute makes the case for hosting a "Christian Seder. He first introduces the festival of Passover and then presents a "Christian adaptation" of it, using this rationale:

 See The Church Resource Institute resource here.[33]

> Our goal here in presenting a Christian adaptation of Passover is to retain the theological, confessional, and educational dimensions of the service. That is, it is presented as a way for people of Christian Faith to express that faith in the context of a gathered community by participating symbolically in the story of salvation. It is presented very deliberately and purposefully as a Christian service, with no apologies. Yet, there has also been a deliberate attempt to preserve the spirit of the Jewish traditions and experience in the service, and to respect the faith journey of

33. QR code URL: http://www.crivoice.org/seder.html.

Israelites and Jews across the centuries. For that reason, apart from the fact that it will likely be Christians who are participating in the service, the thoroughly Christian dimension will come at the end of the service. After all, that is really how God chose to work in history: to the Jew first, and then also to the rest of us![34]

A sixteenth-century fresco of the Last Supper, Kremikovtsi Monastery, Bulgaria. Public domain.

So, in this line of thinking, there is nothing wrong with "adapting" a Jewish Seder to an explicitly Christian context given the faith that Christians and Jews share, and their shared religious history. (One such adaptation suggested is interpreting the *afikoman*—the final portion of the middle *matzah* that has been hidden and is then "ransomed" and eaten to conclude the meal—as the symbol of Christ, using eucharistic bread instead of a *matzah*.)

Three different types of Seders are suggested: the "Full Meal Seder," which is how it is celebrated in Jewish homes, but has the disadvantage of being long and complicated—a challenge for Christians who are trying to incorporate it into a Maundy Thursday service; the "Demonstration Seder," in which only a few elements of the service are shown to an audience and no one actually participates; and the "Symbolic Seder," which falls somewhere between the two previous extremes. It is an example of this latter service that the Website presents, including a Christian Haggadah, which provides a Christian narrative for the service.[35] There are many aspects of this practice that seem problematic to other Christians, leading them to reject the practice of "Christian Seders" altogether.

CON: An Argument against Hosting a "Christian" Seder

Dr. Mary Luti, a United Church of Christ pastor and retired seminary professor, provides one of the most commonly made arguments against Christian Seders in a frequently cited blog post. Her strongest and most serious argument is the way in which a "Christian Seder" either explicitly or implicitly promotes supersessionism: that is, where Christianity is viewed as supplanting and replacing Judaism with a superior understanding of God and God's relationship to humanity in particular. Her concern is that taking a religious celebration that belongs to another and tweaking it in such a way as to make it one's own both violates its integrity and also implies a lack of respect and "power over" that can spill over into other types of Jewish–Christian relationships.

---

34. http://www.crivoice.org/seder.html.

35. http://www.crivoice.org/haggadah.html.

Here is the blog, first posted in 2013 and then reposted in 2014.[36]

The two main problems with this are as follows: first, it makes Judaism a mere precursor to Christianity, encouraging the belief that Judaism's entire function is to herald Christianity (and correspondingly, inaugurate its own destruction); and second, in its worst form, it legitimates anti-Semitism. Here is what Luti says about the latter:

> It is no accident that many a medieval pogrom erupted during Holy Week. It was a time rife with anti-Jewish preaching that placed the blame for Jesus' death on Jews—not just on the ancient Jews, but on all Jews—and, in some cases, directly called for unsparing violence against them. Whenever Christians celebrate a "Christian Seder" that includes or culminates in Holy Communion, it is also chillingly instructive to recall that one of the great medieval slanders against the Jews is that they routinely committed sacrilege against the communion wafer in all kinds of horrific and bloodthirsty ways. This is the history we ineluctably carry with us whenever we do something like celebrate a "Christian Seder." . . . Although holding a Seder (for Christians by Christians for a Christian agenda) may seem like a devout and constructive thing to do, and no doubt for many Christians it lends meaning to the Holy Week journey, it is an unavoidably fraught activity. Our anti-Jewish history has "earned" us a particular responsibility to make sure that our embrace of the Jewish heritage is serious, respectful, self-conscious and well-considered. We may not borrow, play-act, adapt, or otherwise appropriate anything Jewish like a Seder without carrying with us into that activity this whole history.[37]

In other words, either celebrate Passover with Jewish friends and neighbors, or focus on one's own Christian celebrations, and seek to infuse them with renewed appreciation and respect for our Jewish brothers and sisters.

Full disclosure: I find this latter argument compelling; and this is where I stand on the issue. However, I also know other Christians feel and act differently, again, often with the best of intentions. So, to conclude this section, and again, to emphasize the main point I am trying to make in this chapter as a whole—that more interreligious knowledge and dialogue are critically important to make sense of the religiously plural context in which we live and not to give unintended offense—it would, perhaps be helpful here to remind ourselves of what Passover is, and what it commemorates.

36. QR code URL: http://sicutlocutusest.com/2014/04/11/no-christian-seders-please/.
37. http://www.crivoice.org/haggadah.html.

Praxis Point #6

Christian Seders can easily become a huge misstep in Christian–Jewish relations as well as an egregious crossing over from holy envy to misappropriation of another's tradition. Mark Schweizer, in his hilarious and incredibly irreverent "liturgical mystery" *The Baritone Wore Chiffon* (Hopkinsville, KY: St. James Music Press, 2004), recounts the antics of the members of St. Barnabas Episcopal Church in the fictional town of St. Germaine, North Carolina. During one particular Lenten season, the congregation, under the direction of the new rector's wife, hosts an "edible Last Supper" that is meant to be partly a Seder and partly a living recreation of Da Vinci's famous painting. The events in this scene of the book include "authentic" Seder foods such as pork barbecue and pigs-in-a-blanket as well as a Mary Magdalene coffee bar, and the image Schweizer conveys is cringe-worthy enough to steer anyone experiencing holy envy around the Passover meal away from hosting his or her own Christian Seder.

What, then, should Christians do to channel that holy envy into a meaningful and productive Jewish–Christian dialogue? First, get to know members of the local Jewish community and invite them to teach about their ritual. Remembering that imitation is not always the highest form of flattery, do keep in mind that there is nothing wrong with genuine curiosity and a desire to learn more. Entering into relationships with the Jewish community with a sensitivity around this issue and an awareness of the importance of Passover in the cycle of holidays will go a long way in determining the willingness of Jewish neighbors to share their rituals.

At its core, this question of appropriate participation in a Seder meal is a question of relationships. How do we form relationships with our non-Christian neighbors such that they are willing to share of themselves with us? How do we break through the walls that guard us and keep us insulated from creating communities of mutual care and enrichment? The good news is that it *is* possible to build relationships with the "religious other" that are deep and meaningful. The bad news is that this takes time, authenticity, and a willingness to risk being changed. There is an important reciprocity in dialogue that means that one must be willing to share from her own tradition while also receiving from another's. Receiving can sometimes lead to a reassessment of previously held beliefs or positions. This does not necessarily equate to abandoning core convictions, but it might mean letting go of something that is not doctrinal in order to allow room for others to be themselves and to share of themselves.

Seders are a great example of this. Christians have a tendency to read the Last Supper and the eucharistic rite into Seder meals. In so doing, they project Christian particularities onto something that is wholly Jewish. It is sometimes difficult not to do this because those who are tradition constituted are "wired" to see the world through their particular Christian lenses. But, giving up that set of spectacles for one evening in order to participate in a Seder as a Jewish event yields its own rewards of deeper appreciation—appreciation both for the ritual itself and for the friends who opened a window into their lives in order to share it.

Once the relationships have been built that will allow for a sharing of ritual and practice, there are a few things for non-Jews to be aware of in preparing for a Seder invitation:

1. *Seders are long.* There is a lot of history to get through before the eating begins. Dress comfortably and be prepared to wait for the eating portion of the evening. Also, it is a good idea not to make plans for after the event because sometimes Seders can run late into the night.

2. *Meat is a key component of the Seder.* There is also a fair amount of wine. Participants who are vegetarian and/or teetotalers should let the host know about their dietary restrictions well in advance.

3. *Seders during Passover are largely family and close-community events.* Many people treasure these nights and are reluctant have them inundated with strangers or take time away from the holy moment to teach. If members of the Jewish community do not want to open these special moments to non-Jews, do not be offended. Often, people are willing to do demonstration Seders at other times of the year or during other nights in the Passover week.

—*Christy Lohr Sapp*

What Is Passover?

Even though, from the perspective of being from the outside looking in, some might think that Passover is "just" one religious holiday, the fact is that in the shared life and history of the Jewish people, it is so much more than that. George Robinson describes it this way:

> It could be said with some accuracy that the tension between home and exile is central to the Jewish experience. From God's first instruction to Avram, "*Lekh lekha/Go forth on the road*," to the modern Diaspora, to be a Jew has meant to be a transient, in search of a home. To be at home nowhere and everywhere, always to be seeking a return to the Promised Land, to *Eretz Yisroel/the*

The drowning of Egyptians soldiers in the Red Sea. Illustration from *Bible Pictures and What They Teach Us* by Charles Foster, 1897.

Land of Israel, even now, nearly fifty years after the founding of the modern State of Israel.

Nowhere is that tension between exile and home more palpable than in the celebration of *Pesakh/Passover.* The central event of that holiday—the *seder*—is a joyous dinner at home. Yet we try to bring strangers to our Pesakh table (or anyone who does not have a *seder* of their own to attend), a reminder that "you were strangers in Egypt." And the evening ends with the pledge, *"L'Shanah ha-ba'ah bi-Yerushalayim/Next year in Jerusalem!"*[38]

I quote Robinson at length here to remind Christians of the distinctive and special significance this holiday has for Jews in particular; and that while it may, at its core, recount a biblical story that Jews and Christians share, the meaning and significance of that story have a place in Jewish life that is unique and demands its own respect and place.

So, most Christians know that Passover celebrates the exodus story and God's deliverance of the Hebrew people. Specifically, it focuses on the plagues God inflicted upon the Egyptians, particularly the tenth plague—the death of the firstborn sons—from which the Hebrews were spared thanks to lamb's blood spread over the doorposts. In response to this horror, the Egyptian pharaoh demanded that the Hebrews leave Egypt; thanks to Moses' warning, they were ready to leave at a moment's notice. When the Egyptians changed their minds and pursued the Hebrews, God parted the Red Sea for them to cross and drowned the Egyptians when they tried to follow. Everything that is said and done revolves around this story. So, for example, many people have heard that only unleavened bread (that is, bread without yeast) is eaten during Passover (typically *matzoh*); this is because the Hebrews couldn't wait for bread to rise before they fled.

The entire holiday, called *Pesach* in Hebrew, always occurs in the spring and is celebrated over seven or eight days. Different families celebrate it with different levels of observance; but for all Jews it involves a major change in one's diet for the week. Robert Schoen writes: "The Bible and the Talmud tell us that any product that is leavened or fermented may not be consumed during the holiday (this includes bread, cake, cookies, beer, liquor, and so forth). In addition, any food product that is likely to ferment is excluded (including pastas, many types of cereals, and products made from flour). Ashkenazic Jews avoid eating rice as well as beans, peas, legumes, and corn."[39]

The other major aspect of preparation involves "cleaning" the house—but not in the way we typically think. Perhaps a better way to think about this aspect of Passover preparations is "purifying" the house. So, first, the house must be cleared of any leavened products (*hametz*)—all of the food listed above, as well as any crumbs of food. Obviously, historically, for many Jews this could well pose a financial

---

38. George Robinson, *Essential Judaism: A Complete Guide to Beliefs, Customs, and Rituals* (New York: Atria, 2000), 118.
39. Robert Schoen, *What I Wish My Christian Friends Knew about Judaism* (Chicago: Loyola, 2004), 102.

hardship (as well as simply a waste, if all that food were simply to be thrown away). So, non-Jews traditionally have played a role here: for the duration of Passover, this food was "sold" to a non-Jewish family for a nominal sum, in a contract that would be terminated at the end of the holiday. Finally, some Jewish families even have a separate set of cookware, cutlery, and dishes for Passover, swapping out the everyday dishes for these special utensils. Schoen says, "All this may sound like a lot of work and extremely elaborate, and it is. The ritual preparation of a Jewish home for Passover is one of the most stringent spring cleanings you could imagine."[40]

Another key component of the Passover celebration is the *Haggadah*. This is the special book that narrates and orders the Seder meal, and explains the rituals used during the Seder, bringing them to life with different prayers, readings from the Bible, and songs. (Incidentally, if you search online for information about the *Haggadah*, invariably, before you get too far along, someone will mention the "Maxwell House *Haggadah*," which has dominated American Jewish celebrations since it was published in 1932.[41]) There are many, many different versions of the *Haggadah*, written in different times and places to reflect special needs/concerns— and new ones are being written all the time. For example, an interesting New York *Times* article by Jewish novelist Jonathan Safran Foer (published March 31, 2012), explained why he had written a new *Haggadah*: "Our grandparents were immigrants to America, but natives to Judaism. We are the opposite: fluent in 'American Idol,' but unschooled in Jewish heroes. And so we act like immigrants around Judaism: cautious, rejecting, self-conscious, and feigning (or achieving) indifference. In the foreign country of our faith, our need for a good guidebook is urgent."[42] And that is exactly what the *Haggadah* is: a guidebook not only for the Seder itself, but also for the deeper meaning and call to both remembrance and reaffirmation of one's identity that is inextricably embedded in the event.

Finally, the Seder plate must be mentioned. This is a specific—and often ornate—dish that contains the six central symbolic foods eaten in the course of the meal: a hard-boiled egg, which symbolizes the destruction of the First and Second Temples; a lamb shank-bone, which symbolizes the paschal sacrifice offered at the temple; a selection of bitter herbs (often horseradish is used), which recall the bitterness of slavery in Egypt; a sample of green, leafy vegetables, which are first dipped in

The Seder plate. Photo © Yoninah. CC-by-SA 3.0 Unported license (Wikimedia Commons).

---

40. Ibid., 104.
41. You can find an interesting article about this particular *Haggadah* here: http://www.thejewishweek.com/news/new_york/good_last_dayenu. It explains how an updated version, with gender-neutral pronouns and more gender-neutral images for God, was published in 2011.
42. http://www.nytimes.com/2012/04/01/opinion/sunday/why-a-haggadah.html?emc=eta1.

salt water and then eaten—the salt water is said to represent the tears shed in Egypt; another bitter vegetable that also represents the bitterness of slavery; and finally a mix of nuts, chopped fruit, and wine, which is called *Haroset* and symbolizes the mortar used by the Jewish slaves to build bricks in Egypt. In addition, an important part of the Seder celebration is the drinking of four cups of wine, which commemorate the four promises God made to the Jewish people: "I will bring you out," "I will deliver you," "I will redeem you," and "I will take you."

There are many other aspects of the celebration, which can last for hours, and good information is available multiple places online. For example, Jewish Theological Seminary in New York, a Conservative Jewish Seminary, offers a variety of resources, as does Hebrew Union College, a school of Reform Judaism. And, perhaps not surprisingly, there's even an app for that!

 Go here for JTS resources.[43]

 Here for HUC resources.[44]

 And here for the *Haggadah* app.[45]

To wrap up this section, I want to mention one other important overarching aspect of Passover. Schoen writes, "Throughout the recitation of the Passover story we are reminded of our slavery before the Exodus. It is incumbent on each person at the seder to share in the telling as though he or she personally came out of Egypt."[46] Christians must ask themselves how the meaning of that action and those words change in a Christian Seder, and what that change means for the celebration as a whole.

---

43. QR code URL: http://www.jtsa.edu/News/Press_Releases/PASSOVER%E2%80%94THE_STORY_THE_SEDER_THE_CELEBRATION.xml.
44. QR code URL: http://huc.edu/research/libraries/guides/passover.
45. QR code URL: https://itunes.apple.com/us/app/the-haggadah/id504156214?mt=8.
46. Schoen, *What I Wish My Christian Friends Knew about Judaism*, 106–107.

Conclusion

What I have attempted to do in this chapter is offer four concrete examples of interreligious engagement that are happening under our noses, so to speak, and are places where more education and dialogue would be welcome. This education and discussion could go far to shaping healthier Christian conversations and practices. We live in a world that *is* interreligious, in ways both dramatic and mundane, and it is imperative that the education Christians are receiving reflect this reality—and this is true in all educational settings: congregations, colleges, and seminaries. In the next two chapters, I will describe that education more specifically, offering a Christian rationale for interreligious education, and also some of the pitfalls and challenges that it can involve.

What Are Students' Questions?

Kristin Johnston Largen does a wonderful job of laying out several of the pressing issues in this context. I want to dig into her chapters and think about some of the underlying pedagogical issues that arise.

Jane Vella, adult educator extraordinaire, has a useful list of principles to keep in mind when working with adults on learning tasks. It may not be possible to embody all twelve of her list, all the time, but they are a great framework with which to troubleshoot learning. Here's her list:

1. Needs assessment
2. Safety
3. Sound relationship
4. Sequence and reinforcement
5. Action with reflection, or praxis
6. Learners as subjects of their own learning
7. Learning with ideas, feelings, and actions
8. Immediacy
9. Clear roles
10. Teamwork
11. Engagement
12. Accountability[1]

I commend Vella's writing to you more generally, but I want to emphasize that several of these principles (1, 4, 6, 8, and 12, for instance) require that teachers have a sense of what students bring to the task of learning—for instance, what they already know about a topic—and what they hope to learn.

Largen is working off of her extensive experience with seminary students in responding to their concerns. I can "hear" in her chapter the kinds of questions that they often raise. I want to take a moment here to make those questions more explicit, to invite us to listen to students. In what follows I am sharing questions actually raised by seminarians, although I have changed their names to make it possible for me to use direct quotes without violating the Family Educational Rights and Privacy Act (FERPA) rules:

---

1. Jane Vella, *Learning to Listen, Learning to Teach: The Power of Dialogue in Teaching Adults*, rev. ed. (San Francisco: Jossey-Bass, 2002).

The National Association of Colleges and Employers provides a helpful summary of FERPA restrictions in this online article: "FERPA Primer: The Basics and Beyond."[2]

Susan: What kind of Christian public leader do I need to be as I go forward in this world as a preacher who believes she has the word of truth? How must I be shaped by grace so that I can be a light and not a blight in my encounters with people of other faiths?

Sam: Is discussion with people of other faiths about salvation usually destructive? Is it something to avoid? How can these conversations be helpful?

I have had many conversations with Christians about the salvation of those who are not Christian and, often times, these conversations are destructive to at least one person. Is salvation a topic to set aside?

What are some of the spiritual disciplines of other faiths and how do they compare and contrast to disciplines found in the Christian church? How might disciplines of other faiths deepen or broaden my understanding and practice of spiritual disciplines?

Mark: Can we really learn the breadth and depth of the Muslim or Confucian, or Buddhist or any Eastern religion, without learning or experiencing the cultural effect that essentially gives rise to a religion's popularity?

Steve: It's good to serve in tangible ways with those of other faiths, but how do we sit down and hear each other's faith claims? Should we do so, or is that not important in engaging learning with people of other faiths? Let me explain: in the Passion Narratives class, an idea was posed that the way Christians read the Passion accounts would not be accepted in Muslim (and other) circles. Yet, this is one of the foundational stories in the Christian faith. How do we engage one another when there is nuance, contradiction, or some other form of discrepancy? I think these are important conversations to have, but we wouldn't want to step on anyone's toes, nor downgrade anyone's faith or claims.

Alex: I am interested in how we can reach and relate to "dabblers," people who have held multiple beliefs over a relatively short period of time. I am always looking for common points of connection between faiths. In other words, what can I look for in terms of similarities that will bridge faiths?

2. QR code URL: http://www.naceweb.org/public/ferpa0808.htm.

Sharon: Is "love and kinship" truly possible between all faiths from Satanism to Atheism to Wiccaism to Mormonism to Oprahism, etc.? . . . I feel ashamed that a large part of me cannot imagine it being so. Nor can I fathom the countless steps along the journey that need to be taken. . . . I welcome God to meet me in this space and guide the journey that "love and kinship" would increase, that I would grow more at ease as a "guest" and be open to what each encounter brings.

Amelia: Last spring, the adult groups that I lead at my church did a study on world religions. This was an eye-opening experience. One week was devoted to learning about a religion, and the next compared it to Christianity. Most of the people were open and excited about this opportunity. However, I had one woman refuse to even come to the class because she was "happy with her faith and didn't need to learn about any others." This makes me wonder, What was she really afraid of? As leaders, how do we help people feel comfortable about learning and experiencing relationships with people of other religions in a way that helps them be respectful of the differences and at the same time grow in understanding and conviction about their own faith?

Brian: How am I to give an account to another of the hope that is within me? How can I genuinely interact in a mutually vulnerable space and remain secure in my identity, my vocation, and my call? To what degree do I recognize or assume that my ministry field has been inculcated by a hidden agenda, a null curriculum, which tends toward the civic religion? And what am I to do about it? Is it possible to tease apart religion and politics?

Sarah: I hope to learn ways people think and ways in which to handle closed-mindedness in regards to religion. Many of the people I deal with are of the mind that we just do not talk about it. If it is not in the area, why would we need to worry about it? I would like to find a way to discuss, talk, and learn about multifaith aspects in an area that could truly care less about the other in their midst in any form.

Adam: Is it better to be politically correct or authentic when engaging people of other faiths? Do we worry about being offensive to a person of another faith if we are being authentic in our own? (Happy Holidays or Merry Christmas?) How do we address others of different faiths who are struggling with their own faith journey? In particular, if they are in an interfaith relationship, what is our role? Is presence enough or is there more? What can be learned and put into practice from engaging people of other faiths to help those of my own faith tradition that have a negative/destructive view on other faiths to see in a more positive light?

Erick: I'm interested in how we get people to understand different understandings of evangelism that go beyond proselytizing and are more about witnessing in the sense that we are open to what other faiths might teach us about God, and vice versa. How do we help prepare people to have an encounter with other faiths that goes beyond the surface and talks about our real differences in a way that is respectful?

I'm also always struggling with how to talk to other people about how we as Christians are called to relate to people of other faiths without falling into a mass of nebulous pluralism that denies any special meaning to Christianity or to the other faiths.

Are we being presumptuous in suggesting that other faiths necessarily want to have dialogue with us?

Oren: My research and preparation brought up all sorts of discussions about interfaith dialogue and the "anonymous Christian" and religious inclusivism vs. exclusivism. I am excited to learn more about other faiths and people of other faiths and how to humbly be present and accept/ extend hospitality in our neighborhoods. I feel like with many things in theology, there is a balance to be struck between hubris and Christian arrogance and not watering down our belief as Christians that Jesus is our only hope for atonement.

Abraham: How do we, as "Christian" church leaders/educators, help to pass on "the faith" while still allowing people to deepen their knowing of other faiths? Furthermore, what is the line between being open and being considered a universalist? And is that necessarily a bad distinction?

Carol: How do we as Christians obey the Great Commission as recorded in Matthew 28:18-20?

Samantha: My question is, what does it mean to us as Christians to proclaim John 14:6: "I am the way and the truth and the life. No one comes to the Father except through me." What if you aren't so sure? One thing I wonder about is, when we imitate other faith practices, are we being polite or disrespectful?

Amy: Is Christianity the only "true" religion? Does God's revelation of God's self reflect cultural differences such that close investigation leads us all to the same one "true" God (albeit by different names)? What are the commonalities/differences? What is the/a focal point to start discussions?

Peggy: What is this universal need people have always had that causes us to incorporate the practice of religion into our lives? How much of this need is associated with connecting to something bigger than ourselves, and how much of it is associated with our need to connect to one another? Where do our various expressions of religion set us apart from one another, and where do they help us discover what we have in common? What has God been up to throughout history in and through the practice of religion? How are the things that I am learning about other faiths challenging and enriching the convictions I have about my own faith?

I hope that you can hear in these questions the genuine concerns and authentic "wondering" that these students bring to their studies. It is vital to understand that if we, as teachers, are ever to help our students expand and enrich their current understandings, we have to begin from where they are. We have to demonstrate to them that we grasp the internal logic of their concerns, that we have empathy for their starting places.

Faith is, in many ways, a deeply personal and intimate process. Relationship with transcendence inevitably evokes genuine vulnerability, and that vulnerability is only intensified by the structural power differentials of a graduate-school classroom, let alone one that is a crucial step for many students on their journey to being established—being ordained, for some—as pastoral leaders.

When Vella describes the adult learning principles of "safety," "sound relationship," and "clear roles," she is writing in large measure about these kinds of challenges in learning environments, about the very real difficulty of establishing an environment—to use Parker Palmer's words—"in which obedience to truth can be practiced."[3]

Kristin describes in her first chapter a number of instances in which differences in religious worldview led to quite intense public debate via the Web and other forms of social media. Her discussion of whether yoga is an appropriate practice for Christians to take part in, for instance, or whether Christians can and should practice Buddhist forms of meditation, are examples of recognizing the "starting point" of public engagement. Our students are not "blank slates" onto which we can inscribe appropriate content but, rather, living persons who come into our classrooms (whether in person or online) with significant previous experiences. Some of those experiences have shaped their identities, have "written into them" specific ways of being in the world, and when we seek to disrupt those "taken-for-granted" understandings, we must do so with care and compassion.

In several of the student voices I quoted above, you can hear a genuine fear of exploring religious difference. These students are familiar with the heated polarities of public media discourse, and they are loath to wade into such divisive waters. At the same time, they are yearning to find their own voices in ways that express their core convictions. Because they are also familiar with the "dabblers," and the "spiritual but not religious" folk who appear to have little respect for deep religious conviction, these students want to find ways to express their faith that are authentic and have integrity within the traditions from which they come.

For some students, the most pressing of these questions has to do with what Paul Knitter has designated a "replacement" theology in relation to other religions.[4] For some students, the questions arise from an inchoate sense that Christianity must be capable of a response beyond "replacement," but they are not yet aware of

---

3. Parker Palmer, *To Know as We Are Known: Education as a Spiritual Journey* (San Francisco: Harper-SanFrancisco, 1993).

4. I will have more to say about Paul Knitter in my third response section, below.

such an alternative. How are we to meet these students where they are, and then walk with them further down the road of theological discourse and community faith formation? Here I will turn to the second of the points I'd like to make about student learning.

If the first point is that we have to understand where students are coming from, what their questions are, and honor and respect their *current* stances of meaning-making, my second point is that as adults we can invite them to *transform* their meaning-making.

Chapter 2

A Christian Rationale for Interreligious Teaching and Learning

Kristin Johnston Largen

In the previous chapter, I attempted to describe some features of the religiously pluralistic context in which we live today, a context in which I now want to begin thinking about interfaith teaching and learning. More specifically, I want to narrow the focus, describing more concretely what it might mean to teach interfaith engagement in either a Christian college or seminary setting, and why this actually needs to be a central component of religious/theological education today. First, I suggest some of the contemporary issues facing colleges in particular as they think about interfaith education, lifting up three specific dangers that religious education should help students (and faculty members!) avoid. Then, the bulk of the chapter will be spent discussing three specific arguments about why this kind of education is actually of critical importance in higher education—both at colleges and particularly at seminaries.

Three Dangers to Avoid

To get into the chapter, I want to begin with an analogy that I hope will help us describe and better understand what I am identifying as these three key dangers that threaten the healthy expression and experience of religion in daily life today—particularly in the lives of students. So, allow me to introduce that analogy by way of an important theological question: "What's your stance on dogs?"

---

*QR code URL: http://w2.vatican.va/content/francesco/en/apost_exhortations/documents/papa-francesco
_esortazione-ap_20131124_evangelii-gaudium.html.

Personally, I love them: I have a little dog—Henry, my Jack Russell Terrier, the light of my life—and I've always had dogs, and I've always loved dogs. (And, you must know how pleased I am to be able to work Henry into a theological textbook—that doesn't happen very often!) It's a great attitude to have, I think, but it's gotten me into trouble a few times: I always assume dogs are friendly and happy and that they love me—but sometimes they don't, and I've almost been nipped for my presumption more than once.

But perhaps you're on the other end of this "dog–human" relationship, and you don't like dogs at all. They're stinky, they shed, they slobber—and, most importantly, they bite: maybe you've been bitten by a dog yourself, or perhaps you've just read one too many "dog bites human" stories. So, no thanks—you'll stick with your cats, if you please.

OK—so you see the two poles of the spectrum: on the one end are the people who eagerly run to and embrace every dog they see, with equal openness and enthusiasm. On the other end are the people who avoid dogs at all costs, viewing them with suspicion and sometimes outright hostility. Now, in case you haven't realized it already, my point here is not to talk about dogs at all, but instead to overlay these extremes of instinctive human dispositions to an "other" onto a map of various human responses to religious diversity: that is, in the above example, instead of "dogs" read "Islam" or "Hinduism." I argue that when we do that, what we find illustrated for us are the two extremes of *relativism* and *fundamentalism*: two different—and, I would argue, equally unhelpful—ways of viewing and engaging with the religious other. These are the first two dangers that should be avoided.

Relativism

The *Stanford Encyclopedia of Philosophy* (a really great, free online resource, by the way) defines relativism this way: "Relativism is not a single doctrine but a family of views whose common theme is that some central aspect of experience, thought, evaluation, or even reality is somehow relative to something else. For example standards of justification, moral principles or truth are sometimes said to be relative to language, culture, or biological makeup."

 Find the entire definition of relativism here.[1]

In a religious context, then, relativism is the position that all religious beliefs and truth-claims have only subjective, perspectival value: that is, they are relative to the context in which they are held and the specific people who hold them. For the religious relativists, this means that there is no universal standard for determining that

---

1. QR code URL: http://plato.stanford.edu/entries/relativism/.

a specific religious doctrine is true for every-one—or that one view is right and another competing view is wrong. It just all depends on your perspective.

Public domain.

One way of characterizing this group is thinking of them as the "dog-embracers"—those who readily leap into all other religious traditions with open arms, assuming that all religions are fabulous and wonderful, that every religion has something "true" about it, and, since no one can definitively say that one religion is the right one, there is no problem hopping around from one to another: Christianity's good, but so is Hinduism, and Santería and Buddhism and Wicca! These enthusiasts often operate out of the best of intentions, but also often without critical discernment, basic knowledge, and, most importantly, without attentiveness to the particular ground on which they stand.

The reason why this position is dangerous, in my view, is that it promotes the idea that nothing about religious discourse really matters or makes any difference in one's life. That is, it suggests that what religion you participate in is simply a matter of personal choice, and can be put on or discarded like a piece of clothing, without impacting the person underneath. It's like waking up and deciding what to wear: you can wear a striped or a solid tie, black heels or brown ones, and, either way, it's not going to make much difference in the larger picture of the decisions you make that day—how you talk with other people, how you treat them, how you spend your time, and what you care about. And, along the same lines, you can give that tie or that pair of shoes to Goodwill as soon as you decide you don't like them anymore, or they don't suit you anymore, without any significant ramifications. Clothes are window dressing—and personally, I think they are lots of fun—but they come and go, and typically they don't affect who you are as a human being, and how you define and understand your core commitments.

For relativists, the same thing can be said about religions: they might be fun and interesting, but the choice of one religion over another doesn't have any ultimate significance, and no one can really comment on another person's choice—or lack of choice—because it's really whatever suits the mood of each person in a given moment in their life. The problem is that, fundamentally, a religion is not comparable to a piece of clothing. Instead, at their core, religions are meant to provide meaning at the most intense, most critical points of human existence: they answer the question of ultimate purpose, vocation, relationships, and ethics. They are not meant to function as one voice among many, one option on the smorgasbord, but, rather, as the orienting compass upon which all other signs and guideposts are based. When they don't function that way, they aren't able to serve their true purpose of facilitating and shaping human existence and relationships in a positive way.

Fundamentalism

On the other end of the spectrum, we have fundamentalism—the "dog-averse." Now, a definition for fundamentalism is a little harder to come by, because it can mean different things depending on how it is being used. The term originally came out of a conservative Presbyterian movement at Princeton Seminary in the late nineteenth century, which identified five "fundamentals" that were at the heart of Christian belief: biblical inerrancy; the virgin birth of Jesus; the substitutionary atonement theory of salvation; the bodily resurrection of Jesus; and the historical veracity of Jesus' miracles. So, there are many different Christian groups today that self-identify as "fundamentalist"—most of which still hold the above five beliefs.

The term also can be used more broadly, however—it even can be applied to other religious traditions—and in those cases it doesn't refer so much to holding this or that specific belief, but more the intensity and passion of the holding itself. In this more generalized sense, then, "fundamentalism" refers to the position that demands exclusive fidelity to one set of very specific religious claims, with little or no wiggle room. Those in this camp keep a wary distance from all other religious traditions, which are viewed as threatening at best, and actually dangerous and destructive at worst. Many in this camp operate with the best of intentions—wanting only to safeguard the health and security of the religion they cherish—but often this can mean functioning without openness, without humility, and, most importantly, without love.

I think the danger here might be more obvious than with relativism, which often appears rather benign. By contrast, the danger here is at the opposite extreme, which is that the claim a religion makes on one's life is taken to be all-consuming, to a greater or lesser degree cutting one off from the rest of the world and creating the mindset in which anyone who believes differently is considered an enemy— this goes for other religious practitioners as well as other aspects of culture deemed a threat. Fundamentalism often creates a fortress mentality, which encourages people to retreat behind strong walls that do not allow either permeation or conversation with the rest of society—and certainly prevents open conversation with members of other religious traditions. In its most extreme form, it leads to violence—physical, verbal, and emotional.

Interestingly enough, in the Apostolic Exhortation *Evangelii Gaudium* (published in 2013), Pope Francis characterizes both of these extremes as unhelpful, describing fundamentalism as an "obstacle and a difficulty," and what I am calling relativism as "a diplomatic openness which says 'yes' to everything in order to avoid problems."[2] The fact is that neither of these positions is constructive for interreligious learning and growth.

Religious Irrelevance

I'm going to come back to these twin dangers in a moment, but first, a third danger also bears discussion here: the danger of religious irrelevance. If we are going to

---

2. Pope Francis, *Evangelii Gaudium*, ¶¶ 250 and 251.

stick with the dog metaphor with which I began this chapter, these are the people who don't even notice dogs at all: don't care about them, don't pay any attention to them, and can't muster up any feelings at all about them—good or bad. Dogs don't figure into the larger picture of their world, and they aren't a part of their regular reflection about life in general, their decision-making process, their struggle for meaning, and so forth. (Have I pushed the dog metaphor too far? Possibly.)

The point I'm trying to make here is that, for many people, "religion"—either their own faith (if they still self-identify as a religious person) or religious institutions in general—has ceased to have any significance in their daily lives. It's not even that they think religion is "wrong" or "bad," or that they self-identify as atheists. Rather, they just don't think much about religion at all—and see no need to. For whatever reason, they haven't been able to integrate religion into their larger frame of meaning, and its voice isn't one they attend to or value.

We see this phenomenon every day. For example, when it comes to Christianity, there are plenty of people—millions of people?—who have been baptized and even confirmed, some even raised to adulthood in the church, who now see it as hopelessly outdated and narrow-minded, certainly not something that might have anything constructive to offer about the questions of identity, relationship, and purpose that are their most pressing concern. They live every day as though the church simply didn't exist—and for them, for all practical purposes, it doesn't.

Praxis Point #7

We see these people every day. We work with them; we went to school with them; we live next door to them; we are related to them. They are everywhere: the "nones."[3] These are the people who are unaffiliated, unchurched, sometimes atheist—the ones for whom religious belief or practice just does not register. Several years ago, we referred to them as those who are "spiritual but not religious." In 2013, the Pew Research Center[4] found that the United States is in, roughly, a three-way tie between the number of Catholics, white evangelicals, and "nones." This group is on the rise, and many of these individuals are under thirty.

This has implications for interreligious engagement and those with whom we say we are in dialogue. For many students in theological education today, the religious diversity in their communities and ministry contexts will come from this population of "nones." It is important to impress that as individuals build skills in dialogue and interreligious engagement with members of the world's religions, the skills acquired are translatable across various types of difference. The theology that someone articulates that helps her to see the *imago Dei* in a Buddhist or Muslim can also be applied to the spiritual seeker and the spiritual slacker as well.

---

3. QR code URL: http://www.huffingtonpost.com/2014/03/14/religious-nones_n_4956733.html.
4. QR code URL: http://www.pewforum.org/2012/10/09/nones-on-the-rise/.

Oftentimes, it is easier for people of faith to relate to other people of faith regardless of what that faith is. Mere belief engenders a sense of comfort, camaraderie, and familiarity. Thus, it can be unsettling when people who adhere firmly to a faith tradition encounter someone who is simply not wired that way. At those times, it becomes easier to understand the religious extremist than the apathetic agnostic. (I have recently found myself contemplating this question of the "nones" on Easter morning—wondering where people of no faith get their moments of utter joy and transcendence. When the lilies are in bloom, the brass instruments are blaring, and the church is filled with joyful shouts of "He is risen, indeed, Alleluia!," who wouldn't want to share in such bliss?!)

So, the skills of dialogue and engagement can be applied to the "nones" just the same as the Hindus or Jews. Even though there is no tradition to study or tenets to unpack, the "nones" are worth a mention in comparative-theology courses.

It is also worth noting that the atheist contingent is growing, and as this community expands, its need for recognition and inclusion grows, too. There are currently atheist, humanist, or agnostic chaplains at a number of institutions in the United States. There is an ever-increasing call to include the voices of the nonreligious in the midst of dialogue. As scholars and practioners make space for members of "established religions" as dialogue partners, they might also need to consider making room for the atheists and "nones" as well.—*Christy Lohr Sapp*

This is a danger in a different way than the previous two: I am not so judgmental or ignorant (or whatever else it would be) to assume that people who aren't religious are somehow compromised as human beings—that they are fundamentally unhappy or unfulfilled. I'm a Christian, however, so I believe that human beings—all human beings—were created by God for relationship with God, with others, and with the whole world. Therefore, I believe that active participation in a religious tradition (even in those religious traditions that don't believe all human beings were created by God) can deepen and enrich one's life in very powerful and significant ways. Most religions invite individuals into "more": an existence that is about more than just one's daily grind; relationships that are about more than just one's network of friends and acquaintances; and meaning and purpose beyond what one makes of it in his or her own life. So, for me, as a Christian, I believe that life is in some profound and meaningful ways diminished without that dimension.

Scylla and Charybdis

In thinking more about fundamentalism and relativism, I see them as a pair—somewhat ironically, I know, given that they are actually opposite ends of spectrum. However, for just that reason, it is helpful, I think, to hold them in tension, simultaneously avoiding each without sliding too far over to the other as compensation.

As I was reflecting on this dynamic, an image came to mind—that of the paired monsters "Scylla and Charybdis," who found fame in Homer's great epic *The Odyssey*.

As most people know, *The Odyssey* tells the adventure of Odysseus (also known by his Roman name, Ulysses), one of the Greek heroes of the Trojan War who is trying to make it home to Ithaca after the Greeks have sacked Troy and recovered their prize, Helen. What should be a simple voyage ends up taking ten years (in addition to the ten years the war has taken), thanks in particular to the Greek god Poseidon, who never liked the Greeks—and had a special hatred for Odysseus.

Caught between a Rock and a Hard Place, from a sixteenth-century Italian fresco. Public domain.

In the course of his adventures, he must sail through a narrow body of water, which tradition later identified as the Strait of Messina, a slender channel of water that separates the tip of Sicily from the mainland of Italy. No problem for such an experienced sailor, except for one little thing—well, really, two big things: Scylla, a six-headed sea monster on the Italian side of the channel, and Charybdis, a whirlpool off the Sicilian side. The legend told that it was impossible to pass safely through them—you either had to err on the side of Scylla, and lose some sailors to its hungry mouths, or err on the side of Charybdis, and potentially lose your whole ship. (Odysseus, no dummy, chose the former, losing a few mariners in the process, but saving his ship—and himself.)

Here's why I like this image for the topic at hand. Fundamentalism seems to me to present the danger of being swallowed up whole by one particular way of thinking—body, mind, and soul—and doesn't allow for any other options, any other way of viewing the world. And once it gets you, it's loath to let go. Then, on the other side, Charybdis seems to embody well the danger of flitting from one religious tradition to another and another and another, such that you lose all sense of solid ground beneath your feet, and end up being completely confused and entirely rudderless. Once you start swirling down, again, it's hard to get out. And finally, it *is* hard, for all of us, to navigate between these two "monsters," and it's the rare individual who doesn't drift dangerously close to one or the other.

Thus, as a means of going forward in a direction both fruitful and faithful, while navigating a "middle way" between these two obstacles, I want to offer a Christian rationale for appreciative, yet academically rigorous, interreligious engagement that encourages interreligious conversation while at the same time emphasizes one's rootedness in one's own tradition—and the ultimate value such conversation has for that tradition. To make my argument, the rest of the chapter proceeds as follows. First, I begin by saying a bit about the theological discipline in which my work is grounded, comparative theology, and the theological commitments that characterize it. I really have come to value the particular commitments and practices that characterize much of comparative theology, and I think they are worth sharing. Then, I make three claims about the value and, indeed, necessity of this comparative practice that are rooted in the Christian faith itself. Finally, I conclude with a brief epilogue, emphasizing that this is a practice of the heart, not just the head.

Introducing Comparative Theology

So what is comparative theology? James Fredericks defines it this way: "Comparative theology is the branch of systematic theology which seeks to interpret the Christian tradition conscientiously in conversation with the texts and symbols of non-Christian religions."[5] That is, in the Christian context at least, it is a subcategory of Christian theology that does the work of defining Christian doctrines and practices intentionally in conversation with the doctrines and practices of non-Christian religions. So, for example, if one of the main tasks of Christian theology is to articulate who God is and how God reveals Godself to us in any given time and place, the Christian comparative theologian might include as part of that reflection and study the role of the goddess in Hinduism, for example, or the ninety-nine names of God in Islam. The main methodological commitment is that other religious traditions have something important to offer to Christian theological reflection: often it is a fresh perspective, and sometimes it is something new entirely. In either case, however, it is believed that other religious traditions have a unique and valuable contribution to make to the Christian theological enterprise—a contribution that will strengthen and enhance Christian theology, not only for its own sake, but for Christian life in the world.

I recognize that this is, of course, an unusual methodological choice to make. It almost goes without saying that, traditionally, Christians have engaged the theological enterprise primarily with other Christians; and it's only once those core claims have been solidified that non-Christians typically have been brought into the conversation. The clearest evidence one has for this can be found in almost any contemporary textbook of systematic theology. If non-Christian religions are dealt with at all, the standard practice has become to give "religious pluralism" its own chapter (or "Christianity and World Religions")—somewhere in between chapters on Christology and soteriology, or somewhere at the end. That such reflection is there at all is to be lauded, of course, but its placement is meant as something of an interlude, not to disrupt the main line of Christian theological reasoning, typically organized along the structure of the creed.

In another place, I have compared this process to building a house. Typically, Christians rely on Scripture and tradition to lay the foundation and put up the walls of their theological understanding; these are the main chapters of a systematic theology: doctrine of creation, anthropology, pneumatology, and so forth. Only once those fundamentals are place, and once Christian thinking is clear on any

---

5. James Fredericks, "A Universal Religious Experience? Comparative Theology as an Alternative to a Theology of Religions," *Horizons* 22, no. 1 (1995): 68.

given topic, might there be a willingness to experiment with the interreligious "ornamental" aspects of wallpaper and curtains. These "decorative" pieces might improve the look of the place overall, but they don't affect the construction of the house in any way, nor are they in any way instrumental to the whole—they could be removed or changed without any loss of integrity to the structure itself.

By contrast, the comparative theologian seeks to engage non-Christian religions from the very beginning, granting them authority, status, and influence alongside her study of the Bible and reading of important theologians in the Christian tradition. As I stated above, the theological commitment this makes evident is the belief that the practices and doctrines of other religious people are worthy of serious study and reflection, and have something to contribute to the larger Christian theological enterprise.

There is another aspect of comparative theology that I really appreciate, and that is the fact that the final goal of the enterprise goes beyond simply acquiring greater knowledge about the religious other, or even developing better relationships across religious traditions. These are worthy goals, of course, and in places where there continues to be a great amount of mistrust, ignorance, and even hatred of the religious other, better relationships certainly are to be fostered and cherished. For the comparative theologian, however, it is not enough just to stop there. Instead, the comparativist has the lofty aim of transforming her own tradition: applying what she has learned from another to her own understanding of Christianity, such that her own faith is deepened and strengthened in new ways.

Thus, this comparative enterprise presumes two things: first, that those engaging in it come with explicit loyalty to their own tradition, and feel themselves accountable to that tradition. This, then, is not a practice for theological lone rangers or misanthropes. Instead, the comparativist comes to the task well aware of the cloud of witnesses that surrounds her, to whom she is answerable, and on behalf of whom she does her work.

Praxis Point #8

This hearkens back to the idea of being "tradition constituted" that was raised in the previous chapter's comments. The importance of knowing who you are and what you believe is crucial to quality interreligious dialogue, and this cannot be stated often enough. This does not mean that one has to have all of the questions of the universe answered, by any means. It does not mean that interreligious engagement is only for the sages, PhDs, and wizened pastors and professors of theology. What it does mean, however, is that one does a disservice to dialogue when one cannot adequately and authentically represent the tradition in which she stands. It can be confusing for conversation partners and can convey misinformation about one's tradition when one does not remain faithful to one's own tradition.

Sound scary? It should; interreligious engagement is not something to be taken lightly! Dialogue is a weighty act that comes with great responsibility, because in it one is representing not only oneself, but one's entire tradition to another person who, potentially, holds dramatically different worldviews. One often hears a disclaimer in dialogue that suggests that each person is representing only his or her own perspective on a tradition, and to some extent that is legitimate. We all see things in our own ways and represent them accordingly. As tradition-constituted people, however, we each also have a responsibility to represent our tradition as authentically and honestly as possible. This does not imply that one must agree with every aspect of one's tradition, but one should be open and honest about when one is representing a perspective that is a little outside the norm or beyond the mainstream interpretation. To do so simply helps the non-Christian conversation partner to contextualize what she is hearing. And, there is nothing quite like interreligious dialogue to call what we believe into question and to push us to define what we mean by doctrines and commitments that we often throw around without considering them seriously or unpacking them fully.

Once I was in a Christian moral theology class that was pretty evenly split between Christian and Muslim students. The Christians came from a variety of Protestant backgrounds—some mainline and quite liberal, others more conservative and evangelical. The Muslims were all Sunni, quite pious and deeply spiritual. These were all Muslims who took their faith quite seriously but who were eager to learn more about themselves, their own tradition, and their Christian neighbors through this course. The instructor asked everyone who believed in the virgin birth of Jesus to raise their hands. Maybe half of the Christians put a hand up, but all of the Muslims immediately shot their arms straight in the air. Then, the instructor asked everyone who believed that Jesus performed miracles to raise a hand. Again, all of the Muslim hands flew up, and, tentatively, a handful of Christian hands went up—with nervous looks to the left and right. After class that day, a Muslim friend took me aside utterly perplexed by the Christian response to this exercise. He wanted clarity on what is it, exactly, that all Christians believe. What are the basic components that define what it means to be a Christian?

Early on in the comparative theology courses that I teach, I like to share this story and ask that question about Christian belief. Students leave the classroom and continue throughout the semester challenging each other about what it means to be Christian. The core beliefs and commitments are not so easy to pin down and articulate succinctly. Is it adherence to the creeds? Well, not if one is a member of a noncreedal church. Is it the dual nature of Christ? Make sure not to privilege one over the other and to leave room for the Holy Spirit.

Loyalty to a tradition is especially important for students who are preparing for Christian leadership. In many ways, cultivating this loyalty is sewn into the formation process of theological education, but thinking about this in relationship to interreligious engagement is not necessarily part of that process. It should be, and as an increasing number of theological/divinity schools and seminaries recognize the need to prepare Christian leaders to work and serve in a multifaith world, this will be a growing edge of curricular and co-curricular development. In its 2008–2014 work plan, the Association of Theological Schools included interfaith education among institutions' new needs by acknowledging that religious leaders would need to expand their own theologies with a theology of world religions and be prepared to work in inter-religious contexts. The case has been made, and many schools are finding ways to incorporate religious diversity and interreligious education into their curricular options. For a helpful resource, see David Roozen and Heidi Hadsell's edited volume *Changing the Way Seminaries Teach: Pedagogies for Interfaith Dialogue*,[6] published by Hartford Seminary in 2009. This book includes case studies of interreligious courses from several schools.—*Christy Lohr Sapp*

And this leads to the second point: acknowledging the community out of which she comes, the comparativist does her work on behalf of the Christian community as a whole (and, even more specifically, the denomination out of which the theologian comes—the Lutheran church, in my case), such that it is not only her individual faith that is transformed, but the faith of the whole community as well. Noted theologian Francis Clooney says it this way: "The faith of the inquirer cannot be separated from the faith claims of the inquirer's community; this faith is explicitly at issue in the comparative exercise. . . . Comparative theology differs in its resistance to generalizations about religion, its commitment to the demands of one or another tradition, and its goal of a reflective retrieval, after comparison, of the comparativist's (acknowledged) own community's beliefs in order to restate them more effectively."[7]

Now, as I'm sure you can imagine, this practice is not without its own set of risks. James Fredericks notes that the openness to which the comparative theologian is called, and the resulting changes in one's perspective, can be both "disruptive and destabilizing"—and I know that, for many people, this is exactly how it feels. And that's not all: even more seriously, it can feel threatening on a very deep, very basic level. After all, isn't it more likely that a favorable read of and engagement with another religious tradition will weaken one's own commitment to one's faith? Isn't there a chance, even, that such engagement will result in conversion—a person actually leaving Christianity and becoming Buddhist, for example, or Jewish? Well, of course, such things are always possible—anything is possible, and certainly we never can predict the outcome of interreligious engagement 100 percent—that's why it is so exciting and rewarding.

Assuming that one is not just a dilettante in one's own tradition, however—that is, that one actually knows something about one's tradition, actually has a commitment to one's tradition, and, even more, has a living relationship with that tradition—I think it is unlikely. This probably sounds simplistic and even naïve, but I believe that when Christians engage deeply in another religious tradition,

---

6. QR code URL: http://reweb.hartsem.edu/pages/news-events/changing-the-way.aspx.
7. Francis X. Clooney, S.J., *Theology after Vedanta: An Experiment in Comparative Theology* (Albany: State University of New York Press, 1993), 8.

they can trust that the God who has been guiding them all along isn't going to stop now—and certainly isn't going to sulk or abandon someone for engaging in this kind of exploration. Let me be clear: you aren't doing anything "wrong" when you encourage students to open their eyes, mind, and heart to another religious tradition, especially when the motivation for doing so is love of another or, even more, love of the God who created every single person in God's own image, and loves every person, and cares about them. You can reassure both nervous students and nervous parents that God has preserved their faith thus far and certainly will preserve it going forward; and indeed, is likely to lead into new and exciting ways of thinking and acting that they could never have imagined on their own.

Thus, the potential of loss is only one side of the coin. Fredericks goes on to say that, "Although other religions pose a threat to the security of our present theological understanding, they also offer an opportunity for revising those understandings."[8] For this reason, "The comparative theologian is a believer in a crisis of understanding fomented by the intrusive presence of the Other. This means that the comparative theologian operates within a tension defined by 1) vulnerability to the transformative power of the Other and 2) loyalty to the Christian tradition. *All temptations to overcome this tension should be resisted.*"[9]

Those are my italics there, because I can't emphasize that point strongly enough. Oh, I know—who wants to live in the tension? We all hate that, especially in religion! It's so much easier, and feels so much more reassuring, when someone just tells us what is true—what to do and what to think—and doesn't complicate things with shades of grey and multiple perspectives. It would be so much simpler if we could just get all the right answers about our faith, and then just lock them in a drawer somewhere, so we can pull them out whenever we need to make a decision. As we all know, however, the Christian faith doesn't actually work this way, and that's because faith, at its core, is not a dead letter, but a living Spirit that continues to move in our lives in strange and wondrous ways, calling us into new understandings and new relationships. It's certainly not easy—we were never promised easy—but it's rich, rewarding, and powerful; and really, if pressed, would we have it any other way?

Therefore, it's exactly in this tension—this crisis, this vulnerability, and this resistance to minimalizing tense theological reflections—where the exciting work happens. Basically, the argument is that "[Comparative theology] can in non-trivial ways be in harmony with traditional (doctrinal) theology."[10] Even more, comparative theology can actually augment and deepen traditional doctrinal theology.

One of the reasons why I prefer the model of comparative theology (specifically as opposed to comparative religion, for example, which often purports to be value-neutral) is that, in my view, comparing religions should not be an activity for the science lab—that is, where you go in, put different practices or beliefs under a microscope, record their similarities and differences on a chart, and when

---

8. Fredericks, "A Universal Religious Experience?," 86.
9. Ibid., 87, my emphasis.
10. Francis X. Clooney, S.J., *Comparative Theology: Deep Learning across Religious Borders* (Malden, MA: Wiley-Blackwell, 2010), 111.

the experiment is over, you put down your pencil and go home, untouched and unmoved by anything you have learned. Religions are, at their core, expressions of the deepest, most profound human thoughts and emotions, they claim our most passionate allegiances, and they speak a most important word about the truth of our existence. Without being a part of a religious tradition, I think it is much more difficult to understand those commitments in another tradition and thus fully appreciate them. And without being a part of a religious tradition, when there is no possibility for transformation—for you or for anyone else—the comparison becomes a purely academic endeavor; and I think, because of the subject matter, it must be more than that.

Christ and Buddha by Paul Ranson, 1880. Public domain.

What all this means for the rest of this chapter—and really, the book as a whole—is that at its core, it reflects a key theological claim I am convinced is essential for a faithful and relevant articulation of Christian theology in the twenty-first-century global context: Christian theology as a whole is strengthened and enhanced through the engagement with non-Christian religions. And, obviously, Christians themselves are strengthened in their faith, and better able to integrate their faith into the larger context of their lives and have it continue to generate meaning and purpose in ways both fundamental and profound. This is as true for college-age youth as it is for public ministers in training as it is for the average layperson in the pew.

Praxis Point #9

Anyone who teaches courses related to comparative theology or interreligious engagement and dialogue can share myriad stories of how this strengthening and integration are born out in the classroom and in the real world with stories of appreciative students who utilize the gift of dialogue skills far more practically than they do exegesis on Karl Barth's *Church Dogmatics* or abstract ethics. Whether they are serving churches in vibrant, diverse cities, doing hospital or prison chaplaincy, or traveling abroad to work in the mission field, students appreciate the ways in which interreligious engagement challenges them to articulate their own beliefs and find points of appreciation in others' beliefs. In my experience, even those who begin a comparative-theology class reluctantly come to see the value in learning more about themselves through the religious other. Often, students express gratitude for having been given "permission" to step outside of what can come to feel like myopic denominational thinking in order to engage others. This is particularly true when it comes to visiting other places of worship. Time and time again, students comment that this is something they never would have had the courage or motivation to do on their own, but a class assignment became an adventure rather than a drudgery when they suddenly were given a reason to enter a mosque or temple.—*Christy Lohr Sapp*

We Engage in Comparative Theology for the Sake of the Other

For those who are new to this argument—and indeed, new to the whole idea of engaging in interreligious engagement for any purpose other than that of conversion—I think it is helpful to take it in steps, moving from what is easiest to understand and accept to what is the most challenging. So, in that vein, the first step in this argument is that Christians can and should learn something about non-Christian religious traditions for the sake of the religious other; and, in fact, both the license and the mandate to do so rest on a strong biblical foundation. Let me be explicit: there is a Christian religious rationale for engaging in dialogue across religious borders and taking seriously the practices and beliefs of other religious traditions.

In his book *The Immanent Divine*, John Thatamanil writes: "Let me suggest that comparative theology can be understood as motivated by two ancient biblical imperatives: the injunction prohibiting false witness against our neighbors and the deeper injunction to actually love our neighbors."[11] I want to explore each of these imperatives in a little detail, and examine what it might look like to apply them specifically to other religious traditions.

Not Bearing False Witness

Turning to the commandment against false witness, Lutheranism in particular has a treasure in Martin Luther's explication of the Eighth Commandment, as described in his Large Catechism. Luther has one of the most vivid, powerful descriptions of what it means to keep this commandment, which continues to be relevant for us today, as he makes clear that this commandment is not simply about "not-doing"— not gossiping, not slandering—but even more contains within it the exhortation to positive behavior for the sake of the neighbor.

Luther begins by noting how important our good name is for our health and well-being. He writes, "Besides our own body, our spouse, and our temporal property, we have one more treasure that is indispensable to us, namely, our honor and good reputation."[12] Therefore, it is imperative that Christians should do all they can to protect the good name and social standing of their neighbors—and he lifts up particularly the "sins of the tongue" in this context. He therefore counsels Christians not to spread unsubstantiated rumors and not to judge, "For honor and good

---

11. John Thatamanil, *The Immanent Divine: God, Creation, and the Human Predicament* (Minneapolis: Fortress Press, 2006), xi.
12. Martin Luther, "The Large Catechism," in *The Book of Concord*, ed. Robert Kolb and Timothy Wengert (Minneapolis: Fortress Press, 2000), 420.

name are easily taken away but not easily restored."[13] I can't help here but think of the many, many ways Muslims are disparaged in social media—not only in the press, but also in those malicious forwarded emails that circulate like a hydra with multiple heads: so pernicious and so difficult to stop. Luther then goes on to use an extraordinarily powerful metaphor. He writes, ". . . we should use our tongue to speak only the best about all people, to cover the sins and infirmities of our neighbors, to justify their actions, and *to cloak and veil them with our own honor.*"[14] Make no mistake, what Luther is saying here is that if you have any credibility or status in your community: if you are a pastor, a politician, or a business leader, if you come from a powerful family, or even if you just have integrity and a good reputation among your friends, you are to use that social capital on behalf of those who don't have it, and speak up and speak out for them. Luther then concludes his explication with the following:

> Thus in our relations with one another all of us should veil whatever is dishonorable and weak in our neighbors, and do whatever we can to serve, assist, and promote their good name. On the other hand, we should prevent everything that may contribute to their disgrace. It is a particularly fine, noble virtue to put the best construction on all we may hear about our neighbors. . . . There is nothing around or in us that can do greater good or greater harm in temporal or spiritual matters than the tongue, although it is the smallest and weakest member.[15]

Now, of course, we know that Luther himself did not keep this commandment in relationship to people of other faiths—most notably the Jews and the "Turks," as he called them. Nor, frankly, did he keep it in relationship to the pope! However, Luther's own failure to keep this commandment should not dissuade us from taking it to heart in all our dealings with non-Christians, especially in our conversations about them with other Christians. Luther knows that we can do great harm to others without ever even seeing them, or talking with them face to face. All that is required is to confirm the worst about them, or even simply refrain from speaking out when they are maligned. Both of these actions are examples of "bearing false witness," and Christians are called to resist them both.

Loving Our Neighbor

The second mandate we have in the Christian tradition is to love our neighbor. As we all know, there are many, many places in Scripture where this command is reinforced; let me mention only two. First, in the Gospel of Matthew, a lawyer asks Jesus, "Teacher, which commandment in the law is the greatest?" Jesus replies, "You shall love the Lord your God with all your heart, and with all your soul and with all your mind. This is the greatest and first commandment. And a second is like it:

---

13. Ibid., 422.
14. Ibid., 424, my emphasis.
15. Ibid., 424–25.

you shall love your neighbor as yourself. On these two commandments hang all the law and the prophets" (Matt. 22:36-40).

The second example comes from the Gospel of John, in the hours before Jesus' arrest. After Jesus has washed his disciples' feet and is preparing for his betrayal and death, he says to his disciples, "I give you a new commandment, that you love one another. Just as I have loved you, you also should love one another. By this everyone will know that you are my disciples, if you have love for one another" (13:34-35).

These two verses make clear that love is a primary (if not *the* primary) mode of being in which Christians are to live their lives: it suffices as a summary of all the other commandments and prophetic words of the Lord; it is an indispensable core component of fidelity to God; and it is the defining characteristic of one's identity as a follower of Jesus. Elizabeth Johnson writes that since God is present in the whole of the world, "profoundly present and committed to the world and every person in it," "loving God means loving the world." Thus, she writes, "an a-cosmic, unworldly relationship to God is not possible. Encompassed by an incomprehensible holy mystery, we allow our hearts to be conformed to God's own heart, which pours out loving-kindness on the world . . ."[16] Therefore, it can be argued persuasively that it is impossible to love God without loving one's neighbor, and that calling oneself a Christian while hating others (even, as you will recall, hating your enemies) is a fundamental contradiction.

So, how does this relate to one's interactions with members of other religious traditions? I would argue that, typically, when we think about the practice of embodying love, we think about service. This is no surprise, given that Jesus' most famous example of loving the neighbor is the parable of the good Samaritan, and that the way in which Jesus concretized his final commandment to his disciples was to wash their feet. So, one can make a strong case that for Christians, the paradigmatic way in which they express love for their neighbor is by serving them: soup kitchens, Habitat for Humanity builds, hospital and prison visits, and the like. These are of critical importance, and cannot be overestimated. However, I want to argue that there is another, just as valuable way in which Christians are called to demonstrate neighbor-love—and that is through the practice of knowing and being known.

If you are familiar with the work of educator Parker Palmer, you know that this is a topic he discusses in persuasive detail. He begins his book *To Know as We Are Known* with a chapter titled "Knowing is Loving," in which he argues strongly against the model of knowledge that takes "control" as its primary motivation, and instead suggests that "compassion" is at the heart of knowing. He writes, ". . . the act of knowing *is* an act of love, the act of entering and embracing the reality of the other, of allowing the other to enter and embrace our own. In such knowing we know and are known as members of one community, and our knowing becomes a

---

16. Elizabeth Johnson, *Quest for the Living God: Mapping Frontiers in the Theology of God* (New York: Continuum, 2008), 46.

way of reweaving that community's bonds."[17] He goes on to say, ". . . a knowledge that springs from love will implicate us in the web of life; it will wrap the knower and the known in compassion, in a bond of awesome responsibility as well as transforming joy; it will call us to involvement, mutuality, accountability."[18] For Palmer, this act of loving/knowing is grounded first and foremost in the God who knows us and loves us: Christians, first known and loved by God, are thus then called to know and love our neighbors.

Practically, then, what this means is that if you love someone, you want to know something about him: you want to know who he is, what he values, and how he orients his life. If you love someone, you take the time to talk to her, get to know her, and in so doing, you share yourself as well. Love shows itself in attention to another, in accepting another on her terms, in a willingness to learn something new, to think about things a new way, and to grow together in friendship and harmony. When I say Christians are called to love their Hindu, Muslim, Jewish, and Buddhist neighbors, I mean they are called to develop relationships of mutual affection, understanding, and appreciation; this cannot occur without interreligious dialogue.

So this is the first step in the argument, and it is the first place to start, both in practical ministry settings and also in theological education. Both congregation members and candidates for public ministry need to be invited and instructed to engage in dialogue with non-Christian religious traditions, and reassured that such an activity does not mean they are a "bad" Christian, or that they are somehow moving away from—or putting in jeopardy—their life with God. Just the opposite—in fact, this kind of activity demonstrates the seriousness with which they take their own religious commitments, and also their desire to keep religion an active part of their full, rich lives, which quite often includes people of other religious traditions in various ways.

Something Can Be Learned about God

Once this first idea is introduced and people become comfortable with the idea that learning about other religious traditions is actually okay by Christian standards, it's time to move to the second point, which touches a bit closer to home: Christians can and should expect to learn something about God in the course of interreligious exploration; and the basis for such a belief can be found in who God has revealed Godself to be, and how Christians traditionally have understood this divine self-revelation.

Maybe it's obvious how this point is a bit more intimidating than the first. In the previous argument, nothing was being asked of the Christian that might cause her to reexamine her own beliefs or challenge her traditional way of thinking. And that's because the arrow of examination was all one way: the Christian heads out to learn something about someone else, while still being able to keep her own beliefs tucked away safely at home. Now, certainly, it doesn't always work out that way,

---

17. Parker Palmer, *To Know as We Are Known: Education as a Spiritual Journey* (San Francisco: HarperSanFrancisco, 1993), 8.
18. Ibid., 9.

and sometimes (maybe even often) learning about someone else does cause us to rethink our own existence in some way. We don't *have* to, however: learning about someone/something else can remain an external activity that does not touch our own personal beliefs or self-identification. That's what I mean about the arrow just going one way—out from me to another.

Here, however, the arrow of examination isn't just going outward to the neighbor, but also going "up," if you will, to God, and inviting us to learn something new about God—and even rethink our traditional views about who God, how God is at work in the world, and how God is in relationship with humanity. That can be unsettling! And certainly, some Christians will say, "I have the Bible, isn't that enough to learn about God?" And while I believe that we have plenty in the Bible to study for a lifetime, I also think that when it comes to God, there never really is "enough," is there? God is

God Resting after Creation, twelfth-century mosaic from Monreale, Sicily. Public domain.

always greater than we can imagine, more than we can grasp, and revealing Godself in new ways in every time and place. Why not follow that "more" and see what God might be showing us that we hadn't seen before? Again, I know it can be scary, but we have permission—as it were—for doing this from one of the core claims Christians make about God: God is the creator of the whole world, and everyone in it.

God the Creator of All

One of the core, foundational beliefs of the Christian faith is that God is the creator of all: all that exists has come into being through the word and the hands of God; and all that exists relies on the continuing creative activity of God for subsistence moment to moment. Both Augustine and Luther have described this dependence using the metaphor of God's hand constantly undergirding the cosmos; if God were to withdraw God's hand for even an instant, creation would fall immediately into nothingness.

Another common metaphor that expresses this idea is derived from descriptions of the Spirit who moved over the face of the waters at the beginning of creation, the same Spirit breathed into the creature who God molded from the clay, bringing the first human to life. It is this divine aspiration that gives life to all beings; and as God inspired Ezekiel's dry bones, so also is all creation simply parched and withered without the constant flow of God's breath.

Both of these images point to the continued relationship that God has with all God's creatures, and from the existence of this ongoing relationship we can conclude that each creature—human and nonhuman—manifests something of God in his or her very being. In the Bible, this type of revelation is witnessed to in Job, where God answers Job out of the whirlwind, and describes in detail how God's wisdom and might can be seen throughout the created world and the animal kingdom. We also see this repeatedly in the psalmist; for example, in Psalm 19, which reads in part: "The heavens are telling the glory of God; and the firmament proclaims God's handiwork." Theologian Wolfhart Pannenberg echoes this idea when he states that "God's presence permeates and comprehends all things."[19]

Indeed, then, if something of God can be seen and known in creation itself, how much more so must something of God be found in worshipers in other faith traditions, since Christians affirm that every single human being has been created not just by the hand of God but in the very image of God (*imago Dei*). Pannenberg echoes and reinforces this idea, saying that "The inescapability of God's presence by [God's] Spirit means that God is present even with those who turn from [God] . . ."[20]

The great twentieth-century theologian Karl Rahner expresses this idea particularly well. He argues convincingly and powerfully through the use of the concept of the "supernatural existential" that the grace of God is present in and comes to all humans universally, and creates in all of us a searching for God, a longing for God. He writes, ". . . everyone, really and radically *every* person must be understood as the event of a supernatural self-communication of God"—whether or not that communication is accepted.[21] This means that ontologically, fundamentally, and inherently, humans are "oriented towards God"[22] and reflect something of God in their very being.

In the Lutheran tradition, we can look to Paul Tillich, who came to a deep understanding of this idea—and also an appreciation of the consequences of it for interreligious dialogue—at the end of his life. In his forward to Tillich's book *Christianity and the Encounter of World Religions*, Krister Stendahl notes that "After his visit to Japan in 1960, Paul Tillich often said that he felt he should start his theological work all over again."[23] And, in fact, the very last lecture Tillich gave, on the evening of October 12, 1965, was titled "The Significance of the History of Religions for the Systematic Theologian."

In that lecture, Tillich offers a rationale for moving beyond the "true/false" paradigm, by which only Christianity is judged to be true, and all other religions are judged to be false. He grounds his argument on the several presuppositions, of which I want to emphasize two. First, "revelatory experiences are universally human." That is, "There are revealing and saving powers in all religions. God has not left [God]self unwitnessed."[24] The second presupposition is that all humans receive God's revelation in their own finitude and brokenness, which means that

19. Wolfhart Pannenberg, *Systematic Theology*, vol. 1, trans. Geoffrey W. Bromiley (Grand Rapids: Eerdmans, 1991), 411.
20. Ibid., 1:414.
21. Karl Rahner, *Foundations of Christian Faith*, trans. William Dych (New York: Seabury, 1978), 128.
22. Ibid., 53.
23. Paul Tillich, *Christianity and the Encounter of World Religions* (Minneapolis: Fortress Press, 1994 [1963]), vii.
24. Ibid., 64.

revelation is always received in a "distorted form."[25] This comes out of a robust Lutheran doctrine of sin, and points to the need for great humility regarding our own Christian claims. Christians must keep always before them their own weakness and fallibility in interreligious engagement.

Tillich concludes his lecture with a nod to Teilhard de Chardin, and the universality of the experience of "the Holy." Tillich writes, "The universal religious basis is the experience of the Holy within the finite."[26] And because the Holy is present is all religions—depending, in the twenty-first century, how you define the term, I suppose—Tillich argues that the religious symbols of all religions "have something to say to us about the way in which [humans] have understood themselves in their very nature";[27] and when we engage in them, we learn something not only about humanity but about God's relationship with humanity as well.

John Cobb notes that, from this standpoint, "the person who is not a Christian is approached not merely as unbeliever but also as one in whom and through whom the everlasting Word acts and speaks."[28] Thus, Christians can and should expect to find something of God in their encounter with non-Christian religions—how, exactly, God will be experienced, however, can never be predetermined or foreseen. (As another example of this idea, let me mention Raimundo Panikkar's book *The Unknown Christ of Hinduism*, in which he argues for the presence of the God Christians know as Jesus Christ in Hinduism as well—whether recognized as such or not.[29])

Just to be clear: I am not saying all religions are the same; or that all people worship the same God—that is not a necessary, nor even a helpful, conclusion to draw. Instead, I am arguing that on the basis of what Christians confess about God, Christians can and should be open to God's self-revelation in non-Christian religious traditions, and expect to learn something new about God in that engagement. Again, Pope Francis: "Whenever we encounter another person in love, we learn something new about God."[30]

One's Own Faith Can Be Strengthened

Finally, we come to my last point, which is that one's own Christian faith can be strengthened through interreligious engagement. Surely it will be challenged, surely it will be transformed—and there is no guarantee the process will be easy or pleasant. In the end, however, the result of the engagement will be an enriching, an enhancement of one's faith—not a diminishment or a weakening. And with this, the third stage of the argument, we get at the heart of it, and for many, this is the

---

25. Ibid.
26. Ibid., 70.
27. Ibid., 78.
28. John B. Cobb, "The Religions," in *Christian Theology: An Introduction to Its Traditions and Tasks*, newly updated ed., ed. Peter C. Hodgson and Robert H. King (Minneapolis: Fortress Press, 1994), 357.
29. Raimundo Panikkar, *The Unknown Christ of Hinduism: Towards an Ecumenical Christophany* (Maryknoll, NY: Orbis, 1981).
30. *Evangelii Gaudium*, ¶ 272.

line beyond which they will not go. Here, the arrow I spoke of earlier curves back on itself, and demands an examination not just of someone else, or even of God, but of me—my own faith, and my own understanding/interpretation of my own Christian tradition. And this is the most daunting idea of all: perhaps some of the things I have thought about Jesus, about what it means to be a Christian—even some of the things I have cherished most—are wrong, or, at the very least, not quite as unshakeable as I thought they were before, and now I have to wrestle with the ramifications of that. Not everyone is either willing or able to risk such instability and transformation. I understand that. And yet, this really is the most critical move—the one that distinguishes comparative theology from other ways of understanding and engaging in interreligious dialogue; and even though it is the most unnerving, it is also the most rewarding, where the greatest insights are produced and the freshest ideas cultivated. For this reason, it is worth keeping as an aspirational goal, if nothing else.

The Example of the Four Gospels

As perhaps the easiest way into this idea, let me offer a parallel from the Christian faith itself. Have you ever wondered why we have four different Gospels, four different accounts of the life, death, and resurrection of Jesus Christ? It's not entirely self-evident, is it? The fact is, having four Gospels in some ways creates unnecessary problems and logistical headaches for Christians; and especially if you are trying to read the Gospels literally and historically, you quickly run into contractions and complications. For example: Was Jesus born in Bethlehem, à la Matthew, but then later settled in Nazareth, after the flight to Egypt? Or was he born in Bethlehem because of Augustus's registration, as Luke says, and then returned to Nazareth? Or, like both Mark and John imply, did Jesus just "come from" Nazareth originally? And, which was it: A sermon on the mount, or a sermon on the plain? And is it "woe to the rich, full and laughing," or not? And, please, don't even get me started on the crucifixion and resurrection details! All of this confusion would simply have been avoided had the early church fathers simply chosen one—or constructed one—and been done with it.

Eighth-century Irish illumination of an Evangelist surrounded by the four symbols for the Gospels. Public domain.

Actually, there was such an effort in the early church: in the second century, Tatian—a well-known Christian—decided that it was overkill for the church to have four Gospels, especially when there was so much overlap among them. So, he produced a synthesis of the four and called it *Diatessaron*—and it became very popular, particularly in the East. Eventually, however, the Christian community rejected the *Diatessaron*—even though biblical scholar Mark Allan Powell notes that this same approach continues to be employed in our own time, particularly when there is a movie made about Jesus, for example, or a book written about him.[31] Powell writes, "Today, most churches teach that God wanted four people to write four different Gospels and that accepting the Bible as God's word means understanding and appreciating the distinctive stories that each Gospel tells."[32]

   An online version of the *Diatessaron* can be found here.[33]

And certainly, for most Christians, this is the case. It's almost impossible to imagine getting rid of any of them; particularly because we recognize that the picture of Jesus that Christians have come to treasure would be radically different without even one of the four Gospels. For example: get rid of John—it's the latest, after all—but do you really want a story of Jesus' ministry that doesn't include the foot washing? The "Word made flesh"? And I'm not about to give up the woman caught in adultery, either—that's one of my very favorite Gospel stories.

What about Luke? Please—you must be joking: get rid of the annunciation, Zacchaeus, the good Samaritan, the prodigal son? I don't think so. And Matthew? Do you want to lose the genealogy? The wise men? The parable of the vineyard and the day laborers? And Mark—listen, Mark is my least favorite Gospel, but still: the story of Bartimaeus, those brief verses about the guy who runs off naked after Jesus is arrested in the garden—and of course, that cryptic ending: "they said nothing to anyone, for they were afraid."

As Powell writes in another place, each Gospel presents a very different picture of Jesus: Mark is interested primarily in Jesus as the one who died on the cross for sins; Matthew depicts Jesus primarily as the one who abides with his people—founding the church and forgiving sins; Luke shows Jesus as a liberator from oppression, and a savior of the lost; and John describes Jesus as the one who reveals all that can be known of God.[34] Thus, without even *one* of these, we would have a very different picture of who Jesus is and the salvific meaning of his life, death, and resurrection.

---

31. Mark Allan Powell, *Introducing the New Testament: A Historical, Literary, and Theological Survey* (Grand Rapids: Baker Academic, 2009), 99–100.
32. Ibid., 100.
33. QR code URL: http://www.earlychristianwritings.com/text/diatessaron.html.
34. Mark Allan Powell, *Fortress Introduction to the Gospels* (Minneapolis: Fortress Press, 1998), 2.

Vibrancy Enhanced by Engagement

My point is that our picture of Jesus Christ is far, far richer by having more versions of the Jesus story than fewer. It's more complex, sure—more complicated and challenging, too—but it's *better*, because it makes the Christian faith richer, multifaceted, and more vibrant. So, perhaps you have guessed that I want to make a comparable argument with the practice of comparative theology. In an analogous way to what we see in this example with the four Gospels, I argue that a similar richness and vibrancy awaits the Christian—and the Christian faith—through this engagement with the religious other. Similar to how reading all four Gospels—instead of relying exclusively on one—deepens and expands a Christian's understanding of her faith, helping her see Jesus Christ in new and fresh ways, so also to read the Qur'an, for example, or the *Bhagavad-Gita*, gives Christians fresh constructive insights into their own understanding of God, of God's revelation in the world, and humanity's relationship with God.

By way of example, in the fall of 2013, I presented a paper at a Muslim conference on the "Prophethood of Jesus" in Istanbul. For me, it was a great experience to look at how the Qur'an describes Jesus as a prophet, and then go back and rethink the doctrine of the *munus triplex*—Jesus' threefold office of prophet, priest, and king—in my own tradition, which, frankly, has almost entirely suppressed Jesus' identity as human prophet in favor of his identity as divine savior. This suppression has had negative ramifications on what it means to be Christian today and on the larger mission of the church; a renewed emphasis on Jesus' prophethood would be welcome—particularly in Lutheran circles, I think.

So, what I am arguing here is that the different interreligious experiences, conversations, and practices a Christian has will enrich her own understanding and experience of Christianity: they invite her to think new thoughts and imagine new possibilities; and they challenge her deeply held convictions by refracting new colors of light through the prism of her faith. These conversations are not always easy, and sometimes they make us very uncomfortable, as they cause us to see shortcomings in our own cherished beliefs and ramifications of certain views that we were hoping to avoid. But this is a peril that must be faced. Being open to the views and ideas of others is risky, and can be painful, but ultimately, such openness proves to be both rewarding and even indispensable in the end.

Interreligious engagement brings new insights into familiar old stories we thought we knew inside and out, and it brings new life into the dry bones of beliefs and practices on which we had ceased to reflect years ago. And this is true even if we find ourselves holding basically the same convictions after the engagement is over; because, regardless of the conclusions, the process bears its own fruit, providing us with more nuance, more developed arguments, and richer theological interpretation. This is a process we simply cannot do on our own, or even with only those who share our beliefs. We need the religious "other" to produce these fruits.

Conclusion

In his book *Comparative Theology: Deep Learning across Religious Borders*, Francis Clooney writes: "If [comparative theology] does not disrespect doctrinal expressions of truth, neither does it merely repeat doctrinal statements as if nothing is learned from comparative reflection. Rarely, if ever, will comparative theology produce new truths, but it can make possible fresh insights into familiar and revered truths, and new ways of receiving those truths."[35] This, then, is what I work and hope for—an openness to the possibility of fresh insights about one's own faith, as well as new ways of understanding and articulating those insights, not only for one's own theological edification, but for the sake of the church as whole, and the whole human family.

---

35. Clooney, *Comparative Theology*, 112.

How Do We Understand Student Learning as Adult Learning?

Robert Kegan chronicles a model of transformative adult learning that takes seriously the cyclical nature of learning.[1] He describes this as a spiral-shaped path of learning, a process of "confirmation, contradiction, and continuity" that can be endless, but nevertheless spirals forward. "Confirmation" is a process that involves the kind of deep empathy which I have been describing; it involves honoring and respecting where students are when they enter our learning environments. If, for instance, you have learned over your lifetime that to be Christian is to understand Christ's saving power in narrowly exclusive terms, then faith formation can be a process of bringing people to see Christ as the one and only route to salvation. Such a perspective may come to rest in a space in which one's own identity is so narrowly construed that the mere existence of another faith is deeply disturbing, deeply challenging to one's very being, with the logical outcome that one must spend all of one's effort seeking to "impose" such a faith on others. This is not, of course, the only way to understand the salvation that Christ announces! But if students begin from this place, then the process of contradicting their meaning-making, opening it up, challenging it into a larger frame, must also always involve what Kegan describes as "continuity."

For a lovely and brief introduction to empathy, see this RSA animation of a point Brene Brown makes.[2]

What is "continuity" and why is it so necessary? To answer that question, I need to step back for a moment and remind you that human development is a process. You can see that process very vividly with young children. Most children sit up before they crawl, for instance, and crawl before they walk. They will speak in individual words—first names like "Mama" and "Dada"—before they speak in sentences. What is less often recognized is that adults can continue to grow and

---

1. See, in particular, Robert Kegan, *In Over Our Heads: The Mental Demands of Modern Life* (Cambridge: Harvard University Press, 1995); and idem, *The Evolving Self* (Cambridge: Harvard University Press, 1982).
2. QR code URL: http://www.youtube.com/watch?v=1Evwgu369Jw.

develop as well. Our development may be less visible, however, because it is less a matter of mastering ever more fine motor tasks (moving our fingers delicately, or using our tongue and voice to nuance sentences), than it is a task of moving into ever more complex frames of meaning-making.[3]

Perhaps we can see this in the transition the young adults make—or, at least, *can* make—away from constant dependence on their peer group for identity (think of adolescent cliques, or "in-crowd, out-crowd" patterns) to an ability to move between multiple spaces, with appropriate language, behavior, and commitments within specific spaces. I should emphasize here that I am using Kegan's constructive development theory not as a box into which to "put" people but, rather, as a perspective to help us develop deep empathy with and for our students, and the challenges our teaching might create for them.

Development is a process—but, like many organic processes, it can be stopped, or at least starved for growth. When you contradict someone's core meaning-making, you risk sending them fleeing into one of two stances—either fundamentalism (imagine someone "snapping back" into a fierce assertion of their original beliefs) or relativism (which, while it might seem to be the opposite of fundamentalism, is actually quite similar—a "snapping into" a stance where nothing matters, where my meaning is mine, and yours is yours, and neither is better than the other). This "fleeing" is a natural response to feeling threatened. Indeed, as scientists using fMRI machines are learning, even simply disagreeing with an idea can provoke a "fight-or-flight" response.

 For an excellent illustration of this process, see the training workshop offered by the Public Conversations Project, particularly this video.[4]

Largen has explored the problems with either fundamentalism or relativism quite beautifully in her second chapter. What she is offering, when she helps us to walk between the "Scylla and Charybdis" of these two stances, is a path that offers continuity to students.

Asking how we might support authentic adult development that moves beyond the contradictions we propose to our students, or even simply that their lives introduce to them, is a question of how to provide continuity. Continuity is the name for that process by which we come to a new understanding which is connected to our previous way of making meaning, but which grows beyond it. That is, there is "continuity" because we can tell a story, offer a narrative, that respects "from whence we've come" even as it explains "where we are going."

Let me return to the example I used earlier, of a student whose understanding of Christ's presence was embedded in a narrow view of exclusive salvation, a

---

3. Here Kegan's work (see n.1) is my primary source for these assertions.
4. QR code URL: http://www.publicconversations.org/video-series/virtualworkshop/sec1.

view honed and supported by a sense that human action is required to "give faith" rather than a perspective that sees faith as a gift of the Holy One. What kind of understanding of faith might honor that student's commitment to seeing Christ as an exclusive route to salvation, but draw the student beyond narrow forms of impositional proselytism? One possibility—and there are many—would be to help that student recognize that their own conviction of God's power contains within it an answer: that it is God's power at work, not human power. Therefore, trusting in God's gift of faith, in God's overwhelming grace, frees one from responsibility for another's journey, while yet inviting one into wonder and joy at sharing faith.

This is, for instance, one way in which to engage the challenges many people find in the midst of the John 14:6 text: "I am the way, and the truth, and the life. No one comes to the Father except through me." I have preached on this text in various settings, and each time I come back to the same three elements: (1) that it is God speaking, not human beings; (2) that this text speaks to our brokenness as human beings, and when Christians use it to condemn others we only further display that brokenness; and, finally, (3) this is a love so specific, paradoxically, that it is universal. But it is not a love I can control, a love I can embody, but only a love to which I can bear witness. As such, it is welcoming and reconciling, not judging and condemning. This interpretation offers, I believe, a way to find continuity between a Christian stance that affirms God's overwhelming and salvific grace without at the same time creating a judgmental conundrum which requires of us that we impose our current understandings and beliefs on someone else.

Largen has offered us, in several ways throughout her second chapter, rich theological nourishment for contradicting the narrow claims from which many of our students might begin, and drawing them into a deeper, richer, more grounded and centering form of Christian identity.

Chapter 3

Outcomes, Strategies, and Assessment for Interreligious Teaching and Learning

Kristin Johnston Largen

In this third and final chapter of the book, I want to turn to more practical matters, addressing some concrete issues and challenges around the actual implementation of—and engagement with—interreligious education. As a way to get into this, I want to introduce what has become an essential tool for our curricular learning here at Gettysburg Seminary: the ROSA statement. For those of you who are working in theological education, it comes as no surprise that "assessment" is the new watchword for accreditation, and that schools are being nudged/pushed/dragged kicking and screaming into the implementation of more constructive and detailed assessment tools for student learning. The ROSA statement is one way of being explicit about student learning outcomes and the means of assessing those outcomes.

See Gettysburg's statement here.[1]

---

*http://www.clemson.edu/assessment/assessmentpractices/referencematerials/documents/Blooms%20Taxonomy%20Action%20Verbs.pdf.

1. QR code URL: http://www.ltsg.edu/files/5a/5aeff9b5-4f3f-40cf-ae5a-1e6a736db648.doc.

The ROSA Statement

"ROSA" stands for "Rationale," "Outcomes," "Strategies," and "Assessment"; all of our syllabi are now organized this way. Thus, when a student receives a faculty syllabus, she is first presented with a rationale for the course: why this course is being offered, and how it fits with the stated degree outcomes of the institution, for example. Then, she is given a list of outcomes that she should be able to meet when the course is over, and the strategies through which she will develop the capacity to meet those outcomes. Finally, she is given the assessment rubrics by which her ability to meet those outcomes will be evaluated, the different tools that will be employed—tests, papers, participation, projects, and so forth—and the weight each of those will be given in determining her final grade. If it sounds like lots of work for the professors, it is; but the advantage is that it provides real clarity for the students regarding what is going to happen in the course, and why the faculty believe it is important to the larger context of their education—whether seminary or otherwise. In addition, it also provides clarity for the instructors as they navigate the sometimes murky waters of assigning student grades. Finally, in a time in which institutions are increasing being asked to justify both the cost and the length of their programs, this kind of tool enables them to demonstrate the value and role specific courses have in the overarching goals of a curriculum. (Just as a side note, we use the ROSA format for multiple things, including sabbatical proposals, independent studies, faculty planning, and the like. It really is a marvelous tool!)

So, in thinking about the ROSA format as it relates to interreligious education and this chapter in particular, I thought I would attempt to shape the discussion here in the ROSA format—well, really in an "OSA" format, given that chapter 2 was basically an extended rationale for this whole enterprise! What I want to do here primarily is describe some outcomes one might envision for this type of education. In the course of this explanation, I'll also mention some specific resources that I have found useful in my own teaching. From there, I will move to some specific strategies for attaining those outcomes. Finally, in lieu of suggestions for assessing student proficiency in a specific class—a task that each individual professor must establish for herself, in her particular teaching environment—I will offer a few helpful questions that might be asked to assess how interreligious teaching and learning is functioning within and even shaping a particular institution. Let me also reiterate that my own context is a denominational seminary, and thus that is the primary context I have in mind in what follows. However, I think most of what I will describe easily could be modified to fit other settings, for example, a college.

Pedagogical Outcomes for Interreligious Teaching and Learning

Outcome #1: Basic Familiarity

The first outcome that is important for this kind of work is basic familiarity with the religion or religions that are to be a part of the conversation. By that, I mean the ability to remember and describe the core defining practices and beliefs of each tradition—including central sacred texts and general history of a founder (if there is one). To that end, here are a few textbooks that I have found to be particularly helpful out of the multitudes that are available.

 To learn more about Patridge's *Introduction to World Religions,* go here.[2]

First is *Introduction to World Religions,* second edition, edited by Christopher Partridge, which has the advantage of multiple color illustrations, call-out boxes, maps, and timelines, as well as a helpful study companion. The other great advantage of this text—and something, at least to my knowledge, that is unique—is its availability as an interactive textbook (not merely an ebook version), which supplements the full print content with short videos, quizzes, audio clips, slideshows, and more. (Full disclosure: I was the general editor of and a contributor to this interactive textbook, so I'm biased to be sure, but even so, I can testify that it is a dynamic, engaging text, particularly for technologically-engaged learners.) The second text is in the same vein as the first: *World Religions Today,* edited by John Esposito and others. Content-wise, I think this is one of the best out there: it is a dense text with lots of information, but the information is good and clearly explained. Each chapter concludes with discussion questions, a list of key terms, and a short bibliography. It also has maps and timelines.

Both of the previous texts are organized more or less by religious tradition: Buddhism, Islam, and so forth. However, another text I recommend follows a different organizational structure, which, depending on the context, might be more helpful—in an interreligious ethics course, for example. *The World's Religions: A Contemporary Reader,* edited by Arvind Sharma, is organized thematically: Religion and Human Rights, Religion and Women, Religion and the Environment, and the like. Under each of these headings, there are different chapters written by representatives from the different religious traditions, all of which come out of the same conviction: religions "are a *force* in human affairs," which the authors believe can be harnessed for good (even though they also have been—and can be—harnessed for evil).[3] Part 7 is particularly interesting: the heading is "Religion and the Twenty-First Century: Toward a Global Spirituality," and here the authors both acknowledge and in many ways embrace the trend away from "religious" toward "spiritual," and offer a variety of perspectives on how a "spiritual experience" might be defined from different religious perspectives.

---

2. QR code URL: http://store.fortresspress.com/store/product/19264/Introduction-to-World-Religions -Second-Edition-Inkling-Interactive-Textbook.
3. Arvind Sharma, ed., *The World's Religions: A Contemporary Reader* (Minneapolis: Fortress Press, 2011), ii– xiii, http://store.fortresspress.com/store/product/4755/The-World-Religions-A-Contemporary-Reader.

Another engaging text that offers a unique perspective is *World Religions in Dialogue: A Comparative Theological Approach*, edited by Pim Valkenberg.[4] This text only has four parts—Judaism, Islam, Hinduism, and Buddhism—but its great strength lies in what each part contains. Each part is comprised of four chapters: the first written from an "outsider's perspective"—a Christian scholar, but not a practitioner, of the tradition under discussion; the second written from an "insider's perspective"—a scholar-practitioner. Then, the third chapter is on "texts and commentary" from both the insider and the outsider: so, for example, in the part on Hinduism, Aimee Upjohn Light and Madhuri Yadlapati both offer their perspectives on short sections from the Rig Veda, the Upanishads, and the *Bhagavad Gita*, among others. Finally, the fourth chapter offers "concluding reflections" from both authors, and has a more personal, dialogical feel. Given that many Christians end up reading mostly Christian perspectives on other religious traditions, this is a welcome opportunity to hear another religious tradition interpreted by someone for whom it is more than an academic interest.

Finally, *World Religions: The Great Faiths Explored and Explained*, by John Bowker,[5] is the lightest on content, but the heaviest on illustration—the cover promises a "lavishly . . . illustrated book" and it does not disappoint! It wouldn't stand alone very well, but as a companion to one of the previously mentioned texts, it is highly engaging, easily approachable, and a gem for visual learners.

Now, back to the outcome itself. While it might seem straightforward, even basic familiarity can be a challenging outcome in many ways; and of those, I'd like to just mention two. First is the fact that that many students come without any knowledge of other religious traditions, and some might be resistant to doing to the work to gain that knowledge. There are always those students, particularly in a Christian seminary context, who have come to study Christian theology, period, and see any foray into other religions as an unwanted distraction.

Some students may feel threatened by the idea of studying other religious traditions, as they fear, perhaps, that the very act of studying a different religion gives it validity and credibility, and somehow might actually be an "unfaithful" thing to do. What if it is a slippery slope: it begins with innocent reading and discussion, and ends with conversion? I think this is highly unlikely, but of course, it could happen: there always is a chance that learning about an entirely different religious tradition could expose deep insecurities and dissatisfaction with one's own tradition—however, if that were to occur, it is doubtful that this would have been the individual's first intimation of discontent with her own religion! Nevertheless, I want to emphasize that for some students, this fear is very real; and, as I mentioned, it often is coupled with the idea that even the thought of taking another religion seriously is tantamount to discrediting or relativizing Christianity. In an extreme form, this can feel like betrayal to some and blasphemy to others. It is of critical

---

4. Pim Valkenberg, *World Religions in Dialogue: A Comparative Theological Approach* (Winona, MN: Anselm Academic, 2013), http://www.anselmacademic.org/ItemDetail.cfm?ItemNum=7051&tab= ReadReviews.
5. John Bowker, *World Religions: The Great Faiths Explored and Explained* (London: DK Adult, 2006), http://www.goodreads.com/book/show/10284.World_Religions.

importance that, in a classroom setting, students are allowed to voice these feelings and share these fears, even as they are encouraged not to make those feelings absolute. This fear is one reason for some students' reluctance to learn about non-Christian religious traditions.

Another reason for the reluctance, however, has less to do with interest and more to do with practicality: in the current climate when many seminaries are moving toward fewer credit hours and less time to degree completion, it can be hard for some students to justify studying Buddhism, for example, when they feel like an extra preaching course would be more practical in their public-ministry setting. Here, then, is where it can be very helpful to have faculty-wide conversations about how to integrate interreligious learning and teaching into a variety of traditional theological disciplines. When all—or even most—of the faculty support interreligious learning, not only are there various places where students can be exposed to it, but even more, they see the different ways in which it can be integrated into traditionally Christian disciplines. Let me offer just three brief suggestions on how that might occur.

1. Bible Courses

First, in various Bible courses, the sacred texts of other religious traditions might be introduced. Here, I am thinking particularly of the scriptures of Jews and Muslims, where there is both significant overlap and interface—and where there also is a fair amount of ignorance around just what "sacred scripture" in both traditions entails. I don't want to imply that the reading of Buddhist sutras, for example, or a reading of the *Ramayana* or the *Bhagavad-Gita* would not also be constructive and interesting; it is simply that the former is easier for both students and teachers, I think—depending one's personal experience.

Related to interreligious reading of the sacred texts of the Abrahamic faiths, there is a movement encouraging this practice that really has taken off called "Scriptural Reasoning." The practice is defined this way: "Scriptural Reasoning is a practice of inter-faith reading. Small groups of Jews, Christians and Muslims, and sometimes people of other faiths, gather to read short passages from their scriptures."[6] They emphasize that everyone doesn't have to agree, but that the practice deepens understanding and friendship.

 Here is the "Scriptural Reasoning" Website.[7]

---

6. http://www.scripturalreasoning.org/what-scriptural-reasoning.

7. QR code URL: http://www.scripturalreasoning.org/.

The Website offers several helpful resources. The first is a variety of "text bundles"—short texts from each tradition that focus on a theological theme: the first one is "Encountering God," for example. They provide the English translation of all three texts, but then also the Greek, Hebrew, and Arabic originals. They also provide practical guides and videos, and more in-depth academic resources—articles and bibliographic references. Personally, I think in today's context, every public minister should have a Qu'ran on her shelf, and should have at least a basic familiarity of its contents; and being able to lead an adult forum through a comparative reading experience with the Bible and the Qur'an would be a great asset.[8]

2. History Courses

The second place I would suggest integrating interreligious learning is in history courses, inviting students into the interreligious encounters that were happening in different parts of the world, at different times—both for good and for ill. Sometimes, students make the mistake of thinking that interreligious dialogue is a new phenomenon, when, in actuality, the church has been engaging other religious traditions for the whole of its existence. The problem is simply that the knowledge of these engagements often isn't brought to the fore or included in the larger conversation. So, for example, many Christians don't know that there have been many famous Christians scholars over the years who have studied the Qu'ran, including John of Damascus in the eighth century, Peter the Venerable in the twelfth century, and most notably, Nicholas of Cusa in the fifteenth century.[9] The latter's view of Islam was actually quite positive, and even today, Christians have something to gain from studying his work in this area.

The specific example I would offer here comes from close to home, and that is Martin Luther's "engagement" with the Jewish community and faith. I put "engagement" in quotes because of the problematic nature of his discussion, both of

Luther saw non-Christians religions as little more than a negative example against which the superiority of Christianity might be measured. Public domain.

---

8. Here are some good translation options. First, one of the classic texts is *The Glorious Qur'an*, by Muhammad M. Pickthall. The language is antiquated, but it is still standard in many classrooms. Another good option is *The Holy Qur'an* by Abdullah Yusif Ali—this one is very popular. Finally, I have used *Al-Qur'an: A Contemporary Translation*, by Ahmed Ali, which I like. In addition, there are multiple good apps for one's phone. The one I use is "iQuran," and I like it because in addition to having the text in both English and Arabic, it also has the ability to play an audio recitation of each surah, while the English text scrolls along. It is great for students to hear the Qur'an, since it is meant to be recited and heard, rather than simply read.

9. John Kaltner, *Introducing The Qur'an for Today's Reader* (Minneapolis: Fortress Press, 2011), 28.

Judaism as a faith tradition and also of the Jewish people themselves. This is an aspect of Luther's work about which many Lutherans—even many Lutheran pastors—are unaware; and if they have heard vaguely about it, they are convinced it can be isolated and bracketed off from the core of his theology, marginalized as the crabby grousing of a sick old man and certainly not reflective of his biblical thinking in general. This attitude, however, is far from the truth.

Two of my colleagues, Brooks Schramm and Kirsi Stjerna, have published a book that is groundbreaking on this topic. Titled *Martin Luther, the Bible, and the Jewish People: A Reader*,[10] it not only provides new English translations of Luther's major treatises on the Jewish people—including some that previously have been unavailable in English (once you read them, you'll know why!)—but they also situate Luther's anti-Jewish attitude in its historical and theological context.

In their two introductory essays, they not only explain in detail the situation of sixteenth-century Germany (and Europe in general) for European Jews, but they also pointedly challenge the idea that it is a facile business to appreciate and appropriate Luther's theological insights about justification and grace while easily dismissing his anti-Jewish writings. Instead, both come from the same theological roots and are intimately connected; and thus, these writings are something with which every contemporary Lutheran must wrestle. On this point, Schramm writes: ". . . far from being tangential, the Jews are rather a central, core component of his thought and that this was the case throughout his career. If this is in fact so, then it follows that it is essentially impossible to understand the heart and building blocks of Luther's theology (justification, faith, salvation, grace, freedom, Law and Gospel, and so on) without acknowledging the crucial role played by 'the Jews' in his fundamental thinking."[11]

This is, of course, not an isolated example. At almost every point in its history, the Christian church was forced to take account of the different religious traditions with which it came in contact, and make some sense of what the people it was hoping to convert already believed. Many were like Luther, and saw non-Christians religions as little more than a negative example against which the superiority of Christianity might be measured. However, this is only one side of the story. There also were many individual Christians that welcomed this interreligious challenge, and saw it as an opportunity and not a threat. Even centuries earlier, when we might well expect that all Christian missionaries and priests were highly critical of other religious traditions, we can find examples of individuals who were open to learning from other religious traditions and allowed their own Christian practice and beliefs to be transformed by them. This leads to my final example of a place in the curriculum where interreligious could easily be incorporated: classes in Christian mission and global Christianities.

---

10. Brooks Schramm and Kirsi I. Stjerna, *Martin Luther, the Bible, and the Jewish People: A Reader* (Minneapolis: Fortress Press, 2012), http://store.fortresspress.com/store/productgroup/546/Martin -Luther-the-Bible-and-the-Jewish-People-A-Reader.
11. Ibid., 4.

3. Courses in Christian Missions/Global Christianities

Beginning with Christian missionary work, we must acknowledge up front that there are many examples of Christian missionaries who disparaged the religions they encountered and both bullied and threatened the people who practiced them. There are many counterexamples as well, however, but often they are not as well known. If you haven't read him yet, someone whose work in this area you should know is Lamin Sanneh. Currently, Sanneh is D. Willis James Professor of Missions and World Christianity at Yale Divinity School and professor of history at Yale University. Born in Gambia and raised Muslim, he later converted to Christianity. Sanneh's best-known book, *Translating the Message: The Missionary Impact on Culture*,[12] argues that because Christianity translates its Scripture (unlike Islam, which insists on the primacy of Arabic), it also conveys an inherent value and respect on local cultures, and has the built-in capacity to be positively disposed to engagement with the religious "other."

Sanneh describes the African context in depth, and the way in which many missionaries came to see that they were not bringing God to Africa, but that God was already there; and in their adoption of local words and descriptions for God, they were sanctioning indigenous religious beliefs and practices that

Church in Ethiopia. Photo: Giustino. CC-by-2.0 generic license.

were already in place—though sometimes this was not their intention! He also describes early Christian missionary activity to Japan and India. The first phase of missionary activity to Japan, which began around 1570, can be characterized by an attempt to "impose European culture on the Japanese as a price for membership in the church."[13] By contrast, the second phase, which began around 1590, typified a completely opposite approach. The Italian Jesuit Alexandro Valignano imposed a very different standard. Instead of attempting to obliterate Japanese culture, "Everywhere in every possible way everything was to be done in the Japanese fashion and with Japanese ceremony."[14] For Sanneh, Valignano is a perfect example of a Christian missionary who took the translatability of the gospel seriously, recognizing that the Christian message—and its lived reality—was designed to be adapted to and shaped by each culture and language into which it was brought. For this reason, Sanneh describes Valignano's position this way: "Christian mission, he

---

12. Lamin Sanneh, *Translating the Message: The Missionary Impact on Culture*, (Maryknoll, NY: Orbis, 1989), http://www.goodreads.com/book/show/109622.Translating_the_Message.

13. Ibid., 93.

14. Ibid., 94, quoting George Elison, *Deus Destroyed: The Image of Christianity in Early Modern Japan* (Cambridge: Harvard University Press, 1973).

felt instinctively, was vernacular in essence and was thus inherently tolerant of all cultures. Our very difference from others is reason for respecting them as unique bearers of God's universal aim for the human race, not grounds for elevating our own cultural accomplishments as normative for them."[15] For many missionaries, this respect was extended to the other religions with which they came in contact as well.

A great example of this type of missionary activity is the work done in India by the Jesuit priest Robert de Nobili (1577–1656). When Nobili arrived in India, he chose not to set himself apart from the Hindu culture in which he was working and so he eschewed wearing the traditional black robe (if you have been to India, you easily can appreciate how completely impractical and uncomfortable that would have been!); instead, he styled himself after a Hindu *sadhu*, or holy man, and adopted traditional Hindu clothing, even shaving his head. He began an intense study of the local language, Tamil, and eventually mastered Sanskrit and Telugu as well. His methods were controversial, but he persisted. Sanneh describes him this way: "For de Nobili, as for the early Christians, Christianity had not come to uproot but to build upon, not to reject but to renew. . . . he had repeated for Christians in India the transformation that Hellenization had done for the Western Church."[16]

Fr. Robert de Nobili (ca. 1577–1656) was an Italian Jesuit missionary to Southern India and a proponent Hindu-Christian dialogue. Public domain.

Many students are unaware that even four hundred years ago there were Christian leaders who recognized inherent value in difference—even religious difference—and saw it as part of God's plan, rather than an obstacle to it. I argue that these examples (and others like them) can be extremely instructive for students today, informing their thinking when they find themselves in intercultural situations and aren't entirely sure how to respond— let alone what to think about the religious challenge other cultures can pose to Christianity.

Related here are the many contemporary Christian theologians working in an Asian context. (I am focusing on Asia here in particular because one of the well-known characteristics of the Asian context in general is its "both/and" attitude about religions. For example, in Japan, Buddhism and Shinto exist side by side, and no contradiction is seen in having a Shinto wedding and a Buddhist funeral, or having two different home altars next to each other.[17] Thus, for Christianity to insist

15. Ibid., 94–95.
16. Ibid., 101.
17. http://www.buddhanet.net/nippon/nippon_partII.html.

on exclusivity and to view other religious traditions with hostility is profoundly foreign in an Asian culture.) Many of these theologians acknowledge the influence of Buddhism in particular on their Christian faith and practice, and argue the church is richer for it.

One such example is Choan-Seng Song (C. S. Song), a Taiwanese Christian. He is best known for his trilogy "The Cross in the Lotus World": *Jesus, the Crucified People* (1990), *Jesus and the Reign of God* (1993), and *Jesus in the Power of the Spirit* (1994). One of his primary motivations in those texts is to "enflesh" Christian theology in an "Asian body": that is, to indigenize Christian theology so that it is inherently Asian, "born from the womb" of Asia, as it were.[18] In his work, he uses various Buddhist symbols as a way to illuminate Christian symbols with fresh meaning; the most notable example is the way he compares the cross with the lotus, a traditional Buddhist symbol of enlightenment. He also has written a book called *Third-Eye Theology*, where he appropriates the concept of the "third eye" from Zen Buddhism, a symbol of spiritual enlightenment that enables us to see the true nature of being, to describe a way of doing theology more authentic to the Asian context.[19]

Another theologian worth mentioning is Aloysius Pieris, a Sri Lankan Jesuit. (In case you haven't noticed, the Jesuits have a pretty good track record in this area!) Pieris earned the first doctorate degree in Buddhist studies ever awarded to a non-Buddhist by the University of Sri Lanka in Columbo, where he still teaches and writes. One of the particularly important aspects of Pieris's work is the way in which he combines concern for the "many poor" along with the challenge of the "many religions." For him, these are the two main characteristics of the Asian context that Christianity must not only take seriously, but also keep together. In one of the most interesting chapters in his book *Fire and Water*, he asks the question, "Does Christ have a place in Asia?"[20] and goes on to emphasize the way one answers the question depends on *which* Christ is being described. He notes that the "Euro-Ecclesiastical Christ of the Official Church" has been unequivocally rejected in the vast majority of Asian countries; and he proposes instead several different examples of an "Asian Christ," each of which has been influenced by different Asian religious traditions: the Broken Body of the Indian Christ; the Han-Ridden Body of the Korean Christ; the Breast-feeding Christa of Asian Womanhood; and the Third-World Christ of Asia.[21] The discussion here is rich and stimulating.

The last theologian I want to mention is Raimon/Raimundo Panikkar, who died in 2010, and was one of the most interesting and creative voices working in interreligious dialogue in the past few decades. He basically embodied interreligious dialogue in his own person: he held three doctorates, in philosophy, chemistry, and theology; had a background in three different religious traditions, Catholic, Hindu, and Buddhist; he had facility in around twelve languages; and he considered

---

18. C. S. Song, *Theology from the Womb of Asia* (Maryknoll, NY: Orbis, 1986).
19. C. S. Song, *Third-Eye Theology* (Maryknoll, NY: Orbis, 1979).
20. Aloysius Pieris, S.J., *Fire and Water: Basic Issues in Asian Buddhism and Christianity*, (Maryknoll, NY: Orbis, 1996), 65.
21. Ibid., 69–74.

himself both a scientist and a mystic, as well as being a Catholic priest. So, as you might imagine, his theological work defies easy categorization; and, in some ways, I think that is one of his greatest strengths.

Particularly for Western Christians, who often are so eager to nail everything down, separate out truth from falsehood, and make definitive pronouncements—even (and maybe even especially) about God, Panikkar stubbornly insists on God's ultimate mystery, and the need to venture out into new ideas and even new language in order to see reality in a new way. In service of this task, he often coins neologisms—"cosmotheantric" is one of his favorites, as it emphasizes that the world (*cosmos*), God (*theos*), and humanity (*anthropos*) belong together inherently, and one cannot be thought of or described without reference to the other two.

Raimon Panikkar (Panikkar-Alemany) (ca. 1918-2010) was a Spanish Roman Catholic priest and proponent of inter-religious dialogue. Public domain.

Related to this, and one of the points on which Panikkar has been most insistent theologically, is his conviction that ultimate truth—and Ultimate Reality itself—is plural: there is no "common essence" behind all the many names different religions ascribe to God. He insists that "It is a fact that there is a plurality of religions. It is also a fact that these religions cannot be reduced to any sort of unity."[22] Thus, for Panikkar, truth is a "relation," and to even begin to understand and describe it, we need each other: "The 'interfaith' meeting is not just a dialectical affair. It requires love, dialogue, and human touch. We belong together, even if our notions and codes are incompatible."[23]

For this reason, we all have things we can learn from each other, and we all have things we can teach each other—each from our own areas of strength. My colleague Mary Hess, a co-author of this book, actually has the loveliest phrase for describing how this works. Speaking in an ecumenical context, she says that each Christian denomination "tends" things for the sake of the whole Christian communion. So, for example, Lutherans have "tended" the doctrine of justification for the sake of all Christians, while Catholics have "tended" the doctrine of creation and creation's inherent goodness. It's a way both to acknowledge and respect religious differences, and also to recognize that these differences have gifts that bear fruit for the sake of the whole. In this same way, Panikkar would expand this idea beyond Christianity and apply it to the broader family of religious traditions, arguing that the Hindu can teach the Christian about the Spirit, the Buddhist can teach them both about God, and the Christian can teach the Hindu about Christ.

---

22. Raimon Panikkar, *Invisible Harmony: Essays on Contemplation and Responsibility*, ed. Harry James Cargas (Minneapolis: Fortress Press, 1995), 96.
23. Ibid., 99.

Learning and Unlearning

Shifting gears a bit here, I don't want to leave this first outcome of basic familiarity with non-Christian religions without saying something briefly about a second challenge that presents itself with some students when trying to introduce this familiarity. In some cases, it is not so much that students come with no knowledge of another religious tradition, but that they come with knowledge derived from an unreliable (and sometimes even hostile) source, which means before they can learn, they must first "un-learn"—and this often is very threatening, and feels like, to the student, that her opinion and/or experience is not being taken seriously. We all know that it is very easy to get a distorted view of a specific religious tradition depending on one's primary media sources (and one's friends and relatives!), and these opinions can be difficult to dislodge.

Related to this, I can't resist a personal story. I was giving a series of presentations on interreligious dialogue to a group of pastors and laypeople early in 2014, and in the course of one of those presentations, one of the people present said something along the following lines: "I don't know the first thing about Islam—I don't know anything about it at all, but it seems to me that it really is about X, Y, Z." The details are not important: what is important is how this person stated their own complete lack of knowledge about a specific religious tradition, but then in the same breath went on to assert a strong opinion about what it teaches. I hope you see the irony!

I have found that this is not uncommon—even among students—particularly if they have had specific, personal experiences, either in another context, perhaps from living overseas or in the military, or with personal friendships, neighborhood or work connections, and so forth. It often can be very difficult to reframe such an experience, or create a new framework in which a deeper or more nuanced understanding can grow. If someone has a Muslim friend who seems to be dominated by her husband, and lives in such a way that she is allowed very little personal freedom, or if someone has been to India and seen firsthand the negative ramifications of the caste system on lower-caste men and women, it is easy for that one experience to create an overarching critical or dismissive attitude about the religion as a whole which is very difficult to set aside.[24] Conversely, if one has had a great experience with reading a book by the Dalai Lama, for example, or watching a video by Thich Nhat Hanh, that experience can create an equally overarching attitude toward Buddhism that is no less distorted, even though the distortion is positive. Part of the pedagogical challenge of teaching non-Christian religions to Christians is helping them move beyond their preconceptions—whether positive or negative—and being open to learning something genuinely new.

---

24. Among the challenges of interreligious studies is the dynamism of the traditions themselves. However, social media provides some real time opportunities to observe adherents responding to the issues that they currently face. For examples, see: http://www.washingtonpost.com/world/asia_pacific/india-struggles-with-social-media-following-rape-uproar/2013/01/04/7896933e-559a-11e2-89de-76c1c54b1418_story.html; and http://time.com/98770/iranian-women-defy-hijab-law-facebook/.

Praxis Point #10

It is important to emphasize the importance of broad religious literacy in the lives of all citizens but, more importantly, religious leaders. Similarly, it is important to help students understand why a basic familiarity with other traditions will serve them well outside of academia. Let us go back to the unfortunate murder of Balbir Singh referenced in chapter 1. Had the man who shot him known anything about the Sikh tradition, had he known that "Sikh" is not a synonym for "Arab," he might not have pointed his anger in Mr. Singh's direction. At least one life might have been spared.

The unfortunate truth, however, is that many Americans do not have a basic familiarity with their own religious tradition, much less other traditions. Stephen Prothero made this the subject of his highly acclaimed book *Religious Literacy: What Every American Needs to Know—and Doesn't.*[25] I enjoy using Prothero's religious literacy quiz[26] at the start of classes, as an ice-breaker for dialogue, and even when doing religious-diversity trainings with different types of constituencies. Folks are always surprised at what they think they know but cannot recall. Even many Christians have difficulty naming the Ten Commandments and the Catholic Church's seven sacraments. (In this, I am reminded of Charlemagne, who is alleged to have told candidates for baptism to "Go away and learn!" if they could not recite the essentials of the Christian faith, including the Ten Commandments.)

Another technique I enjoy using to help people become aware of the preconceptions and biases they carry about other traditions is an exercise in word association. I have used this, especially, with residence-hall staff at my university. I write words that are often loaded with positive and negative connotations on large pieces of paper and post them on the wall around the room. Then I ask participants to go around the room to each sheet of paper and write the first word that comes into their minds in response to that word or phrase. The reactions to words like "Yoga," "Muslim Woman," "Christian," and "Swastika" elicit reactions that are wide and varied—many of which are addressed in the preceding chapters. An exercise such as this provides an opportunity for interreligious education and learning but, just as importantly, also challenges participants to question their own associations and reactions. This is a great conversation starter for students preparing for religious leadership, as well, as it can shed light on assumptions and prejudices that might be lurking under the surface.

I often find that theological students in particular struggle with perceptions and preconceptions in attempts to articulate their own theologies of engagement with non-Christians. On the first day of class the room pretty evenly

---

25. Stephen Prothero, *Religious Literacy: What Every American Needs to Know—and Doesn't* (New York: HarperOne, 2007), http://www.harpercollins.com/9780060859527/religious-literacy.
26. QR code URL: http://www.pewforum.org/files/2007/12/protheroquiz.pdf.

divides into two categories (using John Hick's classic tri-part typology of pluralism, inclusivism, and exclusivism): pluralists and exclusivists. The pluralists
see themselves as politically correct and more progressive, and the exclusivists
see themselves as upholding the true faith. Nobody wants to be condemnatory,
but in seminary, it is also important to take faith commitments seriously.

It can be a real challenge for students to come to terms with a theology
that resonates with their own traditions—and their candidacy and ordination
review panels—while also maintaining a sense of being hospitable, open, and
nonjudgmental toward the religious other. Yet, it is crucially important for
religious leaders to be able to articulate where they stand in relation to people
of other faith traditions in a way that is in keeping with their home traditions. I call this defining the "non-negotiables" of a tradition and one's personal
faith. As G. I. Joe, the great American hero, used to say, "Knowing is half the
battle!," and in the "battle" for creating a more just, informed, and hospitable
society, knowing more about our neighbors' faith traditions definitely plays a
key role—as does knowing what one's own theology allows and encourages in
terms of interreligious engagement.

I was recently in a Jewish–Christian dialogue in which one participant
turned the conversation to the question of same-sex unions. We live in a state
that recently passed an amendment defining marriage as being between a man
and a woman, only. This person was quite animated that the church needed to
come out strongly on the side of the LGBTQ movement and support same-sex
unions. The Jewish (Conservative and Reform) participants in the dialogue said
that this was not really an issue for their tradition, and then one rabbi made
a comment that really struck me: "I would marry a same-sex couple before I
would marry an interfaith one." The question of interreligious marriage is huge
in the Jewish community, and many rabbis are not allowed to officiate at interfaith ceremonies. Yet, just the opposite is true in many Christian denomina-
tions—marriage to a non-Christian is not problematic but same-sex unions are.
This speaks to the importance of knowing what the non-negotiables are—both
for oneself and for one's denomination.

At the same time, it is important to outline the limits of information being
shared. For example, on the first day of my interreligious divinity-school
courses, I try to make it quite clear that mine is not a comparative religious-
studies course. Students who want a more in-depth survey of world religions
should find that in the religious-studies department and/or in one of the many
resources that are on the market. I see course work, in some way, as helping
students fill their toolboxes of resources from which they will be able to draw
in the future. So, I assign reading that outlines the basic tenets of different
traditions prior to exploring them in a more in-depth way, but I do not spend
multiple lectures on the Buddhist eightfold path or the five pillars of Islam.
I have found that many students do already come to theological education
with a growing exposure to non-Christian traditions. Those who are younger

and coming more directly from undergraduate work have often taken world-religions courses previously or done volunteer service and academic studies abroad. Those who are second-career theological students have often enjoyed workplace or neighborly relationships with non-Christians. Some are returning from military service where they have had the opportunity to serve in a Christian-minority context. As it gets harder and harder to live in religious homogeneity, it also become more incumbent on globalized citizens (as my university aims to create) to have a basic familiarity with "the other."—*Christy Lohr Sapp*

Outcome #2: Enthusiasm and Excitement about the Possibilities

The second outcome I'd like to mention here is less about the mastery of specific information and more about the cultivation of a specific attitude: that is, the conviction that interreligious learning matters, both in Christian academic study and practice/practical-ministry contexts. In my context, where most of my students are preparing for a vocation in public ministry, this is of critical importance, since it will have an impact on how they respond to—and proactively engage—interreligious situations in their settings. This is so significant because, in many places, public ministers provide a model for congregation members regarding what is appropriate action for a Christian when it comes to non-Christian religions; and if the minister is encouraging and enthusiastic about the possibilities, this gives both explicit and implicit permission for lay Christians to respond that way as well.

So, for example, what should a pastor say to a confirmand who has been invited to visit a local mosque with a friend from his soccer team? Should he go at all, and if so, what should he do when he is there? Should he pray with his friend or just watch? Another couple's son is marrying a Hindu woman, and they are concerned about the wedding ceremony: Can they incorporate some Hindu traditions in the service? A young woman passes a Sikh temple every day on her way to work, and one day she sees a notice asking for volunteers to help with their soup kitchen. Is it okay for her to volunteer there, or should she focus her volunteer time with Christian organizations? In each of these instances, there is a moment—an invitation, really—where an individual has an opportunity to say "yes" or "no"—and a gentle nudge in the "yes" direction can make all the difference in the world.

The Ligue d'improvisation montréalaise (LIM) is a league of improvisational theater based in Montreal, Quebec, Canada. © Aude Vanlathem / www.audevan.com.

Excursus: Samuel Wells and Improvisation

Thinking about "yesses" and "nos," I'm reminded of one of the most interesting approaches to Christian ethics I have ever read: Sam Wells' use of the concept of improvisation. There isn't time or space to detail his full argument here, but basically what he is arguing is that the theater practice of improvisation is a good model to use to understand and interpret the "nature and purpose" of Christian ethics.[27] To make his argument, he describes six practices of improvisation that also are helpful in the practice of Christian ethics. Of these, the one that is relevant here is called "Accepting and Blocking"[28]—basically, the difference between saying "yes" and saying "no."

He opens that chapter with a revealing quote from Keith Johnstone, which again is relevant for the conversation here: "There are people who prefer to say 'Yes,' and there are people who prefer to say 'No.' Those who say 'Yes' are rewarded by the adventures they have, and those who say 'No' are rewarded by the safety they attain."[29] I deeply appreciate that Wells is clear that saying "no" does have its own reward, and it's not just about rejection and reluctance to try something new. Instead, saying "no" also is about valuing stability, continuity, and security—all important components both of individual existence and communal life together. Not all "no-sayers" can be properly caricatured as no-fun, stuck-in-the-mud types, who are closed-minded and boring. They also are traditionalists, homebodies, and "conservatives"—in the best (not political!) sense of that word.

He goes on to say that "Communities generally find three kinds of reasons why they prefer instead to say 'No.' They tend to see 'saying Yes' as impossible, improper, or dangerous."[30] Again, this is particularly helpful and relevant here when thinking about interreligious dialogue. For many Christians, these are exactly the reasons why such an activity seems so threatening and unnecessary: it is *impossible*, because religions are so different and there can seem to be so little common ground on which to stand; it is *improper*, because it violates the integrity of their own faith commitments and practices; and, finally, it is *dangerous*, because there is a chance it could weaken their faith, or even lead them into another belief system.

And, let's be honest, even those of us who think that interreligious dialogue is possible, proper, and safe still sometimes tend toward saying "no" to those opportunities—just because they can be a little scary! I know that it is intimating to go to a mosque, even if you are going with a Muslim friend. I know that it takes some courage to cold-call a synagogue and ask if the rabbi would be willing to meet you and host a group of students or congregants. Frankly, it's easier just to stay home! So, I can't emphasize enough that I am sympathetic to those who have a hard time

---

27. Sarah d'Angelo, associate professor in acting in the School of Theatre at Oklahoma City University, delves further into the role of theatre practice for student-center learning in Cari Crumly's Seminarium: Elements book, *Pedagogies for Student-Centered Learning: Online and On-Ground* (Minneapolis: Fortress Press, 2014).
28. The following discussion summarizes the argument in chapter seven of Samuel Wells, *Improvisation: The Drama of Christian Ethics* (Grand Rapids: Brazos, 2004), 103–113.
29. Ibid., 103.
30. Ibid.

envisioning saying "yes" to the many interreligious possibilities that are out there—for whatever reason. And yet . . .

In the language of improvisation, there are two different responses to an "offer" (an invitation to respond) that one actor makes to another in the course of a performance: "accepting" and "blocking." When you accept an offer, you are saying "yes" to their premise, and indicating your willingness to join their game: a child builds a structure with blankets and couch cushions and says to her sister, "Want to come inside my castle?" and she responds, "Sure!," and crawls inside. When you block an offer, you are saying "no" to that premise: "That's stupid—I don't want to play." Now, of course, even Wells says that the point is not to accept all offers all the time—unhealthy, hazardous offers can be proffered, too. However, he does say that "Accepting offers is a practice that builds community by acknowledging, encouraging, and accommodating the other. . . . It requires the sharing of space and implies a continuing conversation about how to go on doing so."[31]

By contrast, "Blocking undermines the other. It refuses to share space and time. It denies outcomes from which all can benefit. It assumes rivalry and enacts conflict in which there cannot be two winners, and most often all are losers."[32] Isn't the imagery of "rivalry" interesting in this context? I think many Christians were raised to believe that there *is* a competition going on; isn't that what missionary activity is all about—"winning" people for Jesus? Christians get nervous when they hear that the percentage of Muslims is on the rise in this country—especially when the numbers of mainline Christians are decreasing. Aren't we "losing"? Shouldn't the church be doing something about that? That kind of attitude naturally leads to more of a "blocking" kind of posture when it comes to interreligious dialogue, a sense that we need to hoard our resources for ourselves, shore up our own walls, and rededicate ourselves to our own renewal: Who has "time and space" to share with others?

This is a fear-based attitude, which many of us can recognize from personal experience: when you are feeling threatened, vulnerable, or weak, who wants to go out to a party? It feels much better to just stay at home. However, what we also all know from experience is that one "no" can easily lead to others: saying "no" can become not merely one decision, but a pattern; and soon enough saying "yes" to any new offer seems unthinkable. And, pretty soon, if you say "no" enough, nobody offers you anything anymore.

Generating Enthusiasm

So, what might be some helpful practical ways of generating the kind of attitude that fosters a "yes" approach—maybe even a "yes, please!" or a "yes, more!" approach? First, allow students to choose their own interreligious dialogue "partner" (and by that, I mean the specific religion they want to explore further) whenever possible. This seems obvious, I know, but it is worth saying, because one can

---

31. Ibid., 108.
32. Ibid.

imagine reasons why a professor might think assigning different students different religions would be best—to guarantee an even distribution of religions in a specific class, for example. However, I would strongly suggest resisting this temptation. In one of the courses I regularly teach on comparative theology, after doing a brief introduction of several different religious traditions (it's necessary to give some level of introductory material, just to give the students some material on which to build further study), I encourage the students to choose the tradition (being as specific as possible—I'll say more about that shortly) that is most appealing to them, rather than dictating which students will study which religions. Inevitably, this means the class isn't as perfectly balanced as I would like (every time I have taught it, Islam is overrepresented), but it means that students have a much higher level of investment and interest than they would have if they were just assigned a specific tradition. I've found there are two primary reasons for this.

First is the situation where a student comes to the class already excited to learn more about one specific tradition—usually because of an experience she has had. A recent example of this is a student who was former military. He had served in the Middle East, and was, of course, exposed to Islam there. Coming back home, he found that people assumed that, as a soldier, he would be very critical of Islam, when in fact, the opposite was true: he had been generally impressed by the Muslims he had met, and was eager to engage in dialogue in his local community. He wanted to compare the things he had heard about Islam anecdotally—both from fellow soldiers and also from the local people he met—with the "official" doctrines of Islam and the way it is described by scholars. In this situation, it would have had a significantly negative impact on his engagement in the course if I had demanded that he study Sikhism, for example, instead of allowing him to follow his passion.

The second thing that often happens is that in the course of learning about a new religion, a student discovers a new practice or belief that they find particularly stimulating and want to learn more about. I hate to use Islam as my example again, but several times in the past few years, one of my Lutheran students has become particularly intrigued by the differences between the concept of "sin" in Christianity and Islam—and the role free will and individual responsibility plays in the latter. They recognize that this is a critical distinction, which has important ramifications about how Jesus is viewed in each tradition, and how believers understand their relationship to God. As a consequence, of course, the students come out with a more nuanced, informed understanding about a Christian doctrine of sin as well, which they typically then are able to articulate and describe better. Again, students do their best work when they are allowed to dig deeper into the areas that have particular meaning for them.

The second pedagogical tool that I've found stimulates student enthusiasm is assigning a project that encourages students to think about how they would introduce interreligious dialogue in their local context. This has several advantages. First, it pushes them to think concretely about ways in which they can connect their academic work with life in public ministry. I am always frustrated when people criticize seminaries for being "out of touch" or "out of sync" with the church as a whole and with "real" congregational life. In my experience, most seminaries care deeply about congregational life, and work hard to make their curriculum both relevant and cutting-edge, such that when their graduates go out in the world, they are well prepared to meet a congregation where it is, but also to lead that congregation pastorally in new directions where necessary. The area of interreligious dialogue is often an area where congregations need such leadership.

Praxis Point #11

This relates to an earlier comment about course work filling a student's "toolkit." Skill with interreligious engagement and dialogue is crucial for religious leaders, and the skills garnered through interreligious activity are translatable across different areas of difference. I try to make assignments practical on this level. So, for example, I will ask students to write/design and share a sermon or Bible study that relates to an interreligious theme or introduces a relatable aspect of a non-Christian tradition. This allows students who are on a parish-ministry track to think about how they might apply the class conversations into their ministry contexts, but it also invites those who are bound for chaplaincy or other forms of ministry to think in advance about the interreligious issues they might encounter.

Case studies are another way to get students thinking practically about how to make room for the religious other in their theologies. I am always amazed at the discussion that grows from the ways in which students say they would handle certain situations. Almost all of the case studies that I use are drawn from real situations (some of which have already been explored in more depth in chapter 1!), and when I share that aspect of the exercise with students, they have a new appreciation for the challenges that might face them. Here are some examples:

- You are the pastor of a congregation and a member comes to you for guidance. She is upset because her son, a young man who you baptized and brought up in the church through Sunday school, youth group, and confirmation, has decided to convert to Islam. How do you counsel her?

- You are the pastor of a congregation and a member comes to you asking to have her wedding in that church, and for you to officiate. She is marrying a non-Christian. Do you perform the ceremony? What are the limitations/expectations you have on such a ceremony? What sort of premarital counseling would you enact? How do you counsel the couple in regards to future child rearing?

- You are working in a hospital as a chaplain. How do you relate to non-Christian patients and their families? How does the conversation change with end-of-life situations?

- You are the pastor of a congregation with ample facilities/space and the local Muslim community approaches you about holding *jummah* prayers in your church. What process do you use to make a decision? In an effort to increase engagement and friendship between the two communities, the imam invites you to speak at a Friday service and asks if he can preach in your service on Sunday. How do you respond?

- You are the pastor of a large church in the downtown area of a respectable-sized town. Your congregation's finance committee has just completed a fundraising campaign to install three new bells in your church's carillon. The carillon is a point of pride in the church and tolls every Sunday morning and every afternoon at five o'clock. Your city's demographic make-up is changing. The local Muslim community has recently built a new mosque. The *adhan* is broadcast prior to prayer, and some neighbors and members of your congregation have begun to complain. They have come to you to support their appeal to the city board to sanction the *adhan*. What do you do?

Such exercises require students to move from the "head" to the "heart" and truly consider what the implications of the course are for their future work. A telling moment emerged in one of my classes when the students who were assigned the interreligious-marriage case study were going on about what conditions they would impose on the theoretical couple before agreeing to marry them. Another student finally had enough of the conversation and said, "I am glad that none of you were the pastor who married my parents, or I never would have been born!" His father is Jewish and his mother is Christian. In our midst was a living example of the case study.—*Christy Lohr Sapp*

So, assigning a project in a course that is focused on dialogue demands that students think critically about their own public-ministry context (for seniors in seminary, this often ends up being the congregation/geographical area in which they are preparing to be called; for middlers—second year students, this can be their upcoming internship congregation), and what sorts of opportunities would best suit the congregations' attitudes and experiences, as well as the local resources. It invites them to be both courageous and innovative, but also realistic and sensitive: what would be interesting and inviting to one congregation could be threatening and off-putting to another; what is possible in a city is not necessarily possible in a rural community. This kind of work gives students an opportunity to experience both the challenges and opportunities around planning and implementing a specific interreligious experience.

In my experience, there have been a variety of good ideas that have come out of this assignment. Some common ideas are a book or film study, a synagogue/temple visit, an adult or confirmation forum, or a guest speaker. One of the most interesting ideas proposed by a student in a recent class was an educational experience that involved listening to chants of various Buddhist sutras, and comparing those with musical settings of different psalms. Again, here students are able to draw from their own personal background and interests, and design an experience they genuinely would like to lead, for a "real" congregation they can envision—maybe even the congregation where they currently worship (this might be true for commuting students, for example, or concurrent interns).

The other advantage that this assignment has is that when students are invited to share their projects with the rest of the class, everyone is able to benefit; and when a project is good enough, other students often will ask for permission to use it themselves. Each student, of course, thinks of things others would not have; and others may have relevant experience that might help tweak a student's project in a more positive direction. And, overall, I have found that the conversation in general is rich and lively, as students begin to envision more concretely all of what might be possible in a public-ministry setting.

It seems to me to be worth repeating that one's own level of enthusiasm and excitement—and one's own disposition as a continual learner—cannot be overestimated in terms of the impact that has on the students. I think it is critically important that they see their professor learning new things—saying, "I don't know," and, "Tell me more about that,"—and being excited about what the students can teach her as a result of their research.

Outcome #3: Confidence and Eagerness to Go Further

Finally, then, the third outcome I would lift up here follows from the second, and that is both the confidence and the desire to continue one's study. The goal is that what happens in a course can provide a springboard to further study and engagement, both for the sake of one's own theological growth, and also for the benefit of the larger church. Of course, it is not possible to mandate "confidence" and "eagerness"—even if a course is intentionally and carefully designed to facilitate those attitudes! Certainly, there will be some students (one hopes a small minority) that come away from such a course with a deepened suspicion of interreligious dialogue, and a greater mistrust of the whole process. The thought of the amount of work that can be necessary to facilitate dialogue in a congregation—patient listening, education, careful building of new relationships, and so forth—some simply will feel it is too much. And, more pointedly, even after the most persuasive education, some public ministers will conclude that interreligious dialogue violates their commitment to the gospel, and their public promise to serve Christ and his church faithfully. If you have read this far in the book, you will not be surprised to hear that, in my view, this conclusion is entirely unwarranted and even untrue—but there is no denying that a percentage of students will both come into and go out of a course in interreligious dialogue feeling this way.

Setting those students aside, however, it is helpful to keep this outcome in mind when planning the course, so that students who are inclined to extend this work further into their public ministry are explicitly and intentionally encouraged to do so. It is important for students who are going into public ministry to be able to explain— to themselves and others—how this deep engagement with other religious traditions, which may well include aspects of a confirmation program, a shared Thanksgiving service, or a joint service project, actually is an important part of the work of sharing the good news of Jesus Christ in the world, and loving God through loving others.

One of the best ways to go about doing this, I think, is imagining where students might hesitate and strengthening them at those points of insecurity and vulnerability. There are two places in particular where such points can occur. First, it is often very intimidating to attend a non-Christian place of worship for the first time—let alone bringing along a group! So, it is very helpful if in the course of a semester students have the opportunity to visit a place of worship and get a sense for the process—how to find a specific community and its schedule of services, whom to contact, what specific accommodations might need to occur for a group, and the like; and also what kind of questions to ask. These include appropriate dress, different components of the service—including the ones in which they would be invited to participate—and the possibility of conversation with community members. I have never had an experience where any religious group has been anything other than whole-heartedly welcoming and encouraging; and very often, the invitation is extended to have a meal and/or additional conversation either before or after the service. Having done this just once, the initial anxiety fades, and students see that this is something they could do, too. Additionally, they feel more confident having some idea of what's going to happen in a particular service, what to wear, how to participate, and so forth.

Praxis Point #12

The visit is a wonderful way to give students exposure to the "lived realities" of other traditions. As mentioned previously, it is important to prepare students properly for such events. Sometimes, students have fabulous experiences and draw deep meaning from others' worship practices. In the reflection papers I read about such visits, I always enjoy it when students share the insights they have gained to their own tradition as a result of the visit. Some even learn a thing or two about hospitality and welcoming the stranger when they allow themselves to be vulnerable in a visit. Sometimes students have challenging visits—such as the time one woman went to a mosque and received a lecture on all of the ways in which Christianity is wrong! Even in these instances, students can come away with a deeper sensitivity for the need for dialogue and charitable assessment of the religious other.

Dialogue experiences in a classroom can often feel forced—especially if a class goes en masse to a prearranged dialogue initiative that is overwhelmed by the sudden influx of eager-to-engage Christians. If a local dia-logue group in town or on campus convenes regularly enough to require student participation, that is great, but often this happens with students as passive observers. As dialogue opportunities are created for students, keep in mind the need for transparency and guidelines from the start. Leonard Swidler's "Dialogue Decalogue"[33] can provide ground rules for engagement, or the group can create its own rules (which often results in greater buy-in).—*Christy Lohr Sapp*

---

33. QR code URL: http://institute.jesdialogue.org/resources/tools/decalogue/.

The Israel-based TRUST-Emun actively promotes interreligious dialogue and community. Used with permission of trust-emun.org.

In the same way, it is helpful to give students the experience where someone from a different faith tradition comes in and speaks—particularly when the speaker is open, friendly, and willing to take every ignorant question thrown at him or her! I have found that there is simply no substitute for being able to engage a Muslim herself—regardless of how much the (Christian) professor knows about Islam. Being able to talk with someone as a fellow believer, and ask that individual about her specific practices and beliefs is an invaluable experience for most Christians— particularly those who have no friends or acquaintances of another religious tradition. People are often skeptical of an "expert"—and one can always find conflicting information on a topic. However, when standing face to face before someone who does not speak about a religion from an academic interest but, rather, from an existential position of commitment and conviction, that testimony cannot be so easily dismissed or overlooked. And again, having experienced it once, they feel much more confident asking someone to come to their ministry context and also are better able to lay the groundwork for such a visit in their own worshiping community.

When it comes to interreligious dialogue, we all are always "on the way," with the destination ever before us and new paths unfolding with each encounter. The instructor should try to avoid conveying the impression that she is "done" and now sits on the mountaintop dispensing her wisdom! Instead, particularly in this case, we are a community of learners, seeking ways to be ever more faithful to the gospel and ever more receptive to the surprising movement of the Holy Spirit. Each class should be a transformative experience for everyone involved—in some ways, for the instructor most of all!

Unavoidable Pitfalls in Interreligious Teaching and Learning

At this point in the chapter, it seems to me helpful to mention briefly three pedagogical hazards that I am calling "unavoidable pitfalls" in teaching interreligious dialogue. They are "dangers" to be sure, in that all three threaten the outcomes listed above either by truncating a student's further intellectual development and growth, or by distorting the integrity and identity of another religious tradition on its own terms. However, they are at the same time "unavoidable," because they typically grow out of exactly the attitude a teacher is trying to foster: enthusiasm and excitement about the enterprise as a whole. So, at least in my experience, you simply can't fully avoid them, but it helps to be ready for them, and prepared to guide students through them and not allow them to stay there and take root. I'll say just a brief word about each.

Unavoidable Pitfall #1: Superficiality

One of the biggest challenges when introducing students to a new religious tradition is to preserve a balance between encouraging them to take ownership of their new knowledge and engage constructively with it, and also helping them to see the vast diversity and complexity that is present within each religion—and stay humble about all they don't know! Just as Christianity resists almost all generalizations about belief and practice—just try to offer a lecture on almost any aspect of Christian doctrine that is equally faithful to both Greek Orthodox and Pentecostal traditions—so, too, other religions have within them sharp and important differences between sects or branches. Some Buddhists think of the Buddha almost exclusively in his historical human existence, while for others, that existence is merely one form among countless others. Some Hindus have deeply personal relationships with one specific deity, while others follow a human guru, and still others worship a variety of gods in accordance with specific seasons, life cycles, needs, and so forth.

Therefore, over and over students must be guided to narrow their field of inquiry. It is not enough to say that one wants to study Judaism, for example. Instead, students must hone their focus as tightly as possible looking at a specific branch, specific texts, and a very specific topic. Typically, over the course of one semester, there is hardly time to even scratch the surface of another religious tradition; and the tendency, of course, is for students to want to say as much as possible about a whole range of things. Over the course of time, however, this ends up leaving them more confused, and also does not give them a good foundation on which to build further study. Better to have a strong grasp of less information than a weak grasp of more information: depth, rather than breadth, will serve them better in the long run. For this reason, it is very important for the professor to keep a balance between breadth and depth in her own teaching—drawing on her own strengths and background, of course. So, for example, when I teach Buddhism, I focus more on the Mahayana traditions, particularly those in Japan, which are related to my own research and writing interests.

Unavoidable Pitfall #2: Overeager Generalizations of Complicated Religious Traditions

Related to this is the second "danger"—the overeager generalization about "what Buddhists believe." Of course, it is important that students feel like they are "getting somewhere" in their study of different religious traditions. They naturally want to feel like they are learning something, and are thus able to speak intelligently about Buddhism, or Hinduism, for example. However, what happens too often is that students take one sliver of information and use it as a base for an all-encompassing theory about religion X. Making generalizations about Judaism based on Reconstructionist Jewish authors, for example, or about Buddhism based on the writings of the Dalai Lama can bring more confusion than clarity. So, again, this tendency needs to be resisted.

Unavoidable Pitfall #3: Natural Tendency to Grasp Onto (and Even Insist On) Commonalities

Finally, the last point I want to mention here is a caution regarding commonalities. For many students, it is both thrilling and deeply gratifying when they come across something in another religious tradition that sounds very similar to something in Christianity. One example that I experienced in a class a few years ago was when a student began studying Shin Buddhism, which, of course, uses language that is often translated as "other-power" and "self-power," and emphasizes complete and total reliance on Amida Buddha for "salvation." This is music to my Lutheran students' ears! They are sure they understand this well, and it makes complete sense to them. (And, of course, I should say, they aren't the only ones: there have been multiple articles written on Martin Luther and Shinran, comparing both the men themselves and their thought, emphasizing their similarities.)

Public domain.

Yet, the rush to compare—even when it comes out of the most laudable instincts: the desire for deeper relationship and common ground, for example—can short-change one's understanding and appreciation of another, and even can perpetuate mistrust, as it can foster the perception that one is not being really "heard" on one's own terms and is instead being folded into a belief system very different from one's own. One might think of Rahner's famous (though often misunderstood) category of "anonymous Christian" in this light: Christians might take great pleasure in concluding that Muslims worship the same God they do, albeit with a different "name," but Muslims, knowing full well what Christians believe about Jesus Christ might not be so eager to rush to that same judgment. (Let me be clear: I'm certainly not ruling that conclusion out, I'm only saying that it needs to come at the end of a long, careful deliberative study process, not at the outset!) So again, the challenge for a professor is to allow students to explore those interesting and exciting points of convergence, without endorsing a smothering of the very real differences and important distinctions in both practice and belief.

Specific Pedagogical Choices and Commitments

Before moving to the final aspect of this chapter, issues of assessment, I wanted to offer just two final suggestions around pedagogy that I have found helpful in my own experience.

Acknowledge Distortions

First, it is important to tailor one's presentations of another religious tradition to an explicitly Christian audience. Even though this creates some level of distortion, it offers a better way into a new tradition, and gives students handholds they can grasp when they are casting around trying to find some anchors in strange waters. In my book, *Finding God among Our Neighbors*, I described the process this way, using an analogy of an interview.

Learn more about Kristin's *Finding God among Our Neighbors* here.[34]

Typically, when people interview someone, they begin by asking specific questions that they think are the most important, the most critical, the best, for getting to the heart of who she is. In the course of that interview, certainly there is no doubt that important information will be received, and an accurate picture of the individual will result. However, think about what might be missed by not allowing the individual herself to narrate the story of her own life: allowing her to choose the topics of importance, allowing her to judge what is and is not significant, and allowing her to speak on the things that are most critical in her eyes. You may well miss some vital pieces of the puzzle, and you may distort other things by describing them out of context: giving some things too much attention, and giving other things too little.

Nonetheless, this is how I typically proceed when introducing non-Christian religions to Christians—even knowing full well the risks. In order to be as clear as possible for a Christian audience, I sometimes have to sacrifice some of each religion's own voice (I hope not too much), telling their story in a way different than they would tell it for themselves (continuing the metaphor). In some ways, this is simply unavoidable: I am a Western Christian writing primarily for Western Christians, and this fact naturally affects the picture I paint of different religions. Thus, it is not the same picture that an insider would paint. One's perspective always influences one's conclusions, and all scholars, particularly scholars of religion, must be transparent about that fact. It is my hope that, after their introduction, students will seek out other sources of information, particularly texts and/or personal

---

34. QR code URL: http://store.fortresspress.com/store/productgroup/585/Finding-God-among-Our -Neighbors-An-Interfaith-Systematic-Theology.

contacts from within these traditions, so that the unique voices of these religions might be heard on their own terms.[35]

Focus on Essentials

Second, particularly in a seminary context, one simply must expect to spend a fair amount of time on Islam, given the current context and the kinds of interreligious questions/situations in which public ministers will expect and find themselves— then Judaism, then Buddhism, then Hinduism. This is not because these four religions are more important than others, but because these are likely the religions with which Christians will be coming in contact, and about which Christians will have questions. (This is also why I made the choices I did in chapter 1). My hope is that this is changing, and will continue to change over time, but at least in the recent past, it has been my overwhelming experience—when I am out in congregations and also having conversations with my own students—that the greatest misconceptions, and thus the greatest need for dialogue and education, are centered on Islam. As I mentioned in a previous chapter, I would go so far as to say that in a twenty-first-century United States context, every public minister must have at least a rudimentary understanding of Islam and a basic familiarity with the Qur'an, simply to be able to advise helpfully and pastorally lay Christians who are desperately in need of some guidance on what to think and say about Muslims. This is no less true about the other religions I mentioned, either—it's just that anxiety is *so* high here, and misunderstandings *so* significant, that the need for good information and faithful Christian discipleship seems so critically important. Thus, in my experience, Islam should always have an important place in the larger context of interreligious classes/conversations.

Muslim prayer beads. Photo: James Gordon. CCA 2.0 Generic license (Wikimedia Commons).

Transforming Assessment

Normally, for assessment, one has specific tools that one uses to evaluate student learning outcomes, like research papers or the project I described above. Those tend to be context- and content-specific, so the professor needs to develop them in the framework of the particular course one is teaching. Therefore, here I thought it might be helpful to suggest some larger questions that could be asked, not only

---

35. Kristin Johnston Largen, *Finding God among Our Neighbors: An Interreligious Systematic Theology* (Minneapolis: Fortress Press, 2013).

regarding the experience of individual students, but of faculty members as a whole, and even of an institution. For me, these questions get at the heart of what I see as the larger goals of interreligious learning and teaching—not only transforming individuals who take part in those educational abilities, but the transformation of the institutions that support them, and through them, the transformation of society as a whole. (Just a modest little aim, I know!)

So, keeping that in mind, here are some larger kinds of questions one might engage to evaluate both the ongoing oversight and also the ultimate success of these sorts of learning environments. First, starting with the students themselves, it is helpful to survey recent alumni, asking them for their assessment of the interreligious component of their education when they are some years out of the institution. Of course, current students should be invited to give evaluations of specific courses while they are still at the institution, but it also is important to see how they regard and reflect upon those courses/experience once they are engaged in their own professional lives. Are they incorporating anything they learned in their own professional ministry, or teaching, or even in their personal faith lives? Have they come to regard that work as more or less valuable over time? How did it prepare them for life in the world—and how did it not? This also helps remind the faculty that their work is not intended to focus simply on the semester at hand, but it seeks to form a specific kind of individual who takes interreligious education to heart, and actually lives it out in a variety of ways in her own life.

Second, regarding the institution itself, it is helpful to ask about how well the faculty as a whole is able to integrate issues of comparative theology and dialogue into the curriculum more broadly. Again, the idea here is not to add one discipline among many to an already full plate of academic competencies. Rather, ideally, the overarching goals of interreligious teaching and learning are that they be embedded into a variety of disciplines, including extracurricular activities, such that both the students and the faculty have multiple points of exposure, and multiple opportunities for constructive integration.

Finally, thinking also intuitively but beyond it as well, one might assess the kinds of networking connections that have been made through one's institution into the community. Are there connections between local worshiping communities, where students are invited to participate and congregants are invited, in kind, to the institution? What about local service organizations, especially those that already have an interfaith component? How does one's institution interface with other local interfaith efforts? These questions and others like them can help an institution, and individual faculty members, create and nurture the best possible kinds of interreligious learning environments, which serve students well both in the short term and the long term.

How Do Theologies of the Pluralism of Faith Help?

Kristin Largen notes, early in her chapter 3, that even basic familiarity with other religions can be a challenging outcome for students, particularly those whose identities feel threatened by engagement with different faiths. While I agree with the rich examples and suggestions she makes there—particularly about the utility of work with a ROSA for a course—I want to dig more deeply into this issue of students feeling threatened or challenged. Having "set the stage" with a discussion of "confirmation, contradiction, and continuity," I can now use that framework to help us work with even those students who feel most threatened.

I want to use that frame for exploring the work of one particular theologian who has offered concrete strategies for exploring religious pluralism from a Christian perspective. The theologian is Paul Knitter, and the work that I want to explore here comes from one of his later books, *Introducing Theologies of Religions*.[1] In that book he works carefully through four specific responses from within Christianity to the clear evidence of vitality within other religions.

While I agree with Largen in her articulation of the "unavoidable dangers" of superficiality and overeager generalization, remember that these dangers stem in large measure from students seeking to connect new learning with previous learning. That is, we know—from the neuroscience of learning, as well as from long experience with master teachers—that it is much more difficult to disrupt previous learning than it is to "lay down" new synapses. And one element of laying down new channels of learning is to connect them with previous channels. Hear again the importance of "confirmation, contradiction, continuity."

Part of what makes Knitter's book so compelling is his careful exploration of the four "frames" he engages. People who hold each of these frames feel that he has represented well what their stance entails. Such a representation is rare in public religious contexts. As you can hear in the student quotations I offered earlier, many of our students have encountered religious differences not as an invitation to deeper dialogue and richer complexity but, rather, as yet another example of people not listening well to each other.

We can talk all we want about having an "Eighth-Commandment" stance—that is, not bearing false witness, or even better, to use Martin Luther's terms, putting the "best construction" on our neighbor's views—but many of our students have

---

1. Paul Knitter, *Introducing Theologies of Religions* (Maryknoll, NY: Orbis, 2002).

very little actual experience with such a process. Therefore, Knitter's careful explanations of each of four Christian stances toward other religions—replacement, fulfillment, mutuality, and acceptance—offer a remarkably unique approach. He explores each model, identifying what he terms insights from the model and articulating questions which arise in the context of that model. In doing so, he offers an example of a theological-inquiry stance that invites deeper engagement and inevitably draws out student thinking in richer, more complex ways.

Let me offer a brief summary of his process here, by way of direct quotations from his work (page numbers in parentheses).

The Replacement Model

Insights

- The centrality of the scripture for Christian life (50)
- The reality of evil and the need for help (51)
- Jesus as the One and Only (53)
- Beware of religion (55)

Questions

- What to do when there is a clash between what the Bible says about other religions and what other religions say about themselves? (56)
- If we grant that there are two sources for a Christian theology of religions—both the Bible and the dialogue with other religious believers—is it possible to understand this one-and-only language differently than have Christians in the past? (59)

The Fulfillment Model

Insights

- Truth and grace in other religions (100)
- Dialogue essential to Christian life (101)
- Nonnegotiables in all religions (102)

Questions

- Does the fulfillment model really allow dialogue? (103)
- Does commitment require certitude? (104)
- How does Jesus save? (105)

The Mutuality Model

Insights

- The need for new answers (150)
- Jesus as sacrament (152)
- A Spirit Christology (154)
- A Christology of mutuality (156)

Questions

- A creeping imperialism (157)
- A creeping relativism (162)
- Is it really Christian? (164)

The Acceptance Model

Insights

- We are all inclusivists (216)
- The value of differences (219)
- Dialogue has the right-of-way to theology (222)

Questions

- Is language a prism or a prison? (224)
- Can many salvations save our world? (229)
- Many absolutes = No absolute? (232)
- Can comparative theology be "theology-free"? (235)

I hope you can begin to catch a glimpse here of the way in which Knitter works at theological inquiry. In addition to providing a respectful and nonjudgmental entry point into each stance, he offers a set of compelling questions which, at least in my experience, have invited students to name their own engagement in these issues. This kind of process is very much part of what Jane Vella identifies as a principle of "engagement" and "learners as subjects of their own learning."

Of course, engaging these stances and drawing students into articulation of their own reflections on such theological frames poses its own set of challenges. Many of the students with whom I have worked on this material are frustrated by not knowing which of these stances is Knitter's own stance, personally—or which of the stances is the one that I, as the teacher, find most compelling. Yet another of the "preexisting" understandings, or "confirmation of their stance" that we must engage stems from far too many of our students being shaped by an educational system that encourages "teaching to the test" rather than "testing the teaching."

Here is where Largen's third chapter is both astute and strategically effective. Across the landscape of higher education we are moving toward more explicit commitments to ongoing assessment. Students who have grown up in a world of high-stakes tests and rigid accountability have learned to seek out, early in a course, an instructor's specific desires with regard to their assignments. Indeed, far too many of our students have submerged their own inquiry and interest under an overriding concern for "discovering what a teacher wants and when he wants it." While the use of rubrics and other forms of assessment can err on the side of such mechanistic learning, they can also be used to help students open up to new possibilities. I find Grant Wiggins and Jay McTighe's framework for the "six facets of understanding" very useful in this instance, because they offer a rubric that assesses understanding in terms of perspective, empathy and self-knowledge, in addition to more common categories of explanation, interpretation, and application.[2] What would it mean for us to concern ourselves explicitly with a student's growth in her perspective, empathy, and self-knowledge?

 For more on the "six facets of understanding," see this link.[3]

I believe that Largen is attending to these elements, if only implicitly, when she writes that ". . . it is helpful to keep this outcome in mind when planning the course, so that students who are inclined to extend this work further into their public ministry are explicitly and intentionally empowered to do so. . . . One of the best ways to go about doing this, I think, is imagining where students might hesitate and strengthening them at those points of insecurity and vulnerability." I hear a clear sense here of the need to walk alongside of students—to confirm their reality—at the same time as you invite them into further journeying. Kristin offers a number of ways to do this, ranging from sharing the work of specific theologians, to discussing practical ways to invite people into your classroom—and to taking your students into "classrooms" that are in communities. I agree with her that it is vitally important to practice "engagement with" rather than merely "teaching about" specific religions and experiences of faith, in part because of the epistemological shifts our wider contexts are undergoing.

I have written at length elsewhere about what a "new culture of learning" consists in, given the pervasive spread of digital technologies, so here let me simply note three dynamics that are shifting rapidly and are deeply implicated in our learning about other faiths: how we understand authority, what we mean by authenticity,

---

2. See Grant P. Wiggins and Jay McTighe, *Understanding by Design*, exp. 2nd ed. (Alexandria, VA: Association for Supervision and Curriculum Development, 2005).
3. QR code URL: http://www.slideshare.net/drburwell/the-six-facets-of-understanding.

and how we practice agency (both individually and collectively).[4] The days are rapidly disappearing in which it was possible for a professor to make an assertion in the classroom and have it accepted purely by virtue of their structural role as instructor. While those of us who are professors might find that shift challenging, it is a deeply adaptive response on the part of our students. It is impossible to live in today's society without keeping at least one strong antenna attuned to the validity and authority of the information you engage.

Kristin writes about the specifically damaging ways in which Islam has been represented—not only in fictional film and television, but in the so-called objective news. Part of what we need to do is help our students to build a critical perspective as they engage the world. Such a perspective, however, does not, can not, and should not stop at the doors of our classrooms. Who speaks for a particular religion? How do we who are not of that religion discern an answer to that question? I am reminded both of how important it is to have an adherent of a religion interact with my students—and how difficult it is to choose wisely who might be an appropriate "spokesperson."[5]

Part of why I find Knitter's work so compelling is that he is able to demonstrate what a stance of wonder might be in relation to specific Christian stances.[6] Might we also offer such a stance of wonder toward multiple instances of a particular religious tradition? Here Largen's advice about asking students to focus their work very specifically in just one corner of a larger tradition is very pragmatic, because it also narrows the range of options toward which one might direct oneself in wonder. I live and teach in the Twin Cities of Minnesota, and I have learned through experience with multiple respondents that what it means to be a Muslim from Turkey is quite different from how a Muslim from Somalia understands her faith and tradition.

Beginning to recognize the multiplicity of stances in another religion is often only possible once one can see—even embrace—such a multiplicity in one's own home space. Yet, far too many of our seminary students come into our classrooms with a need to prune multiplicity, rather than to perceive it, because living in the midst of multiple perspectives is too challenging to their own identity. Here again, Knitter is helpful because he invites people to see how perceiving diversity within Christianity does not need to be threatening, but can be, instead, a powerful way to deepen one's own commitments. He offers, to return to Robert Kegan's formulation, a form of continuity that can ground contradiction in a deeper, more

---

4. See, for instance Mary Hess, "A New Culture of Learning: Digital Storytelling and Faith Formation," *Dialog* 53, no. 1 (Spring 2014): 12–22; and idem, "A New Culture of Learning: Implications of Digital Culture for Communities of Faith," *Communication Research Trends* 32, no. 3 (2013): 13-20.

5. Perhaps here it is also important to remember that asking someone to speak of their faith as a "representative" of a larger whole puts them in a difficult position. As the only Roman Catholic teaching on a Lutheran faculty, I know something of what it means to be pushed into the role of spokesperson. It is in many ways inevitable, but the deeper goal, the longer-term goal, ought to be to invite students into ongoing relationships with multiple members of a specific community of faith.

6. I should emphasize here that Knitter's typology is only one of many, and even Knitter himself does not argue that it is definitive. My use of his work must emphasize that it is his underlying respect for difference in the context of Christian thought which is the pertinent point in this response.

thoroughgoing approach to one's faith. I am reminded of the tagline of a project of the Minnesota Council of Churches—the "Respectful Conversations Project"—which invites people into respectful conversation around divisive topics by assuring them that the goal is *not* to "change people's minds" but, rather, to "soften their hearts."[7]

Still, determining what is authoritative for a particular tradition in a particular context is a challenging exercise, and the more provisional one can be about the formulation, the more grounded and authentic its reception. Indeed, part of the shift that is occurring in terms of how we understand authenticity grows out of this recognition that authority has to be nuanced, and the more strongly a specific authority is asserted the more problematic and inauthentic it might be.

Here is where Largen's assertion that, in addition to basic familiarity, we ought to be seeking her stated outcomes of "enthusiasm and excitement about possibilities" as well as "confidence and eagerness to go forward" resonates so strongly with me. Much of what is being learned by researchers who are studying the impact of digital technology on learning points to the importance of "inquiry-driven" and "project-based" learning. I have already mentioned the destructive formation of learning that is occurring in some schooling contexts, but here I can point to the constructive formation of learning that is taking place in a variety of digital contexts. Mizuko Ito, danah boyd, Jane McGonigal, and many others have delineated the ways in which children and young adults are drawn into complex, focused, and challenging learning in the midst of their play—whether the play is that of multiuser online games like *World of Warcraft* (a game that frequently showed up in research), or varieties of other learning environments structured to facilitate creativity.

See, for instance, the work funded by the MacArthur Foundation on digital literacies.[8]

Excellent educators have long known that to shape *depth* learning we must make an impact on emotion and physicality. The cognitive alone is not enough; we need to work with the affective and the psychomotor as well. New research in neuroscience only confirms this insight, making it all the more crucial that we draw on pedagogical practices that give us access to the "epic adventures" of which McGonigal writes, or the "accepting and blocking" moves that Largen draws on from improvisational theory.[9] One "side effect" of this kind of emotionally engaged, physically active, and cognitively rich learning is that it conveys authenticity in ways that learners socialized into digitally rich spaces find compelling.

7. http://www.mnchurches.org/respectfulcommunities/respectfulconversations.html.
8. QR code URL: http://www.macfound.org/programs/learning/.
9. For an excellent introduction to neuroscience and teaching, see James Zull, *The Art of Changing the Brain* (Sterling, VA: Stylus, 2002).

Seminary faculty ought to recognize this insight, because, unlike some contexts of higher education, we teach and learn in places in which embodied learning is sought, and we have elements of such learning throughout our subject areas. While teaching about liturgy or preaching may be the most obvious of such topics, when we draw students into the rich history of traditions, or help them to parse the contextuality of biblical interpretation, we are often able to do so by the multisensory and multivocal nature of our materials. Certainly, any intent to do formation requires such a recognition.

And here the final element of the three I noted earlier—authority, authenticity, and agency—becomes particularly pertinent. What it means to "have agency" in the midst of learning is a complicated and contested question, but in digital cultures it is an inescapable one. Largen gives a particularly useful pedagogical example of why it is important for students to have agency in their learning when she writes about why she invites students to choose a religion to explore that interests them, one in which they feel their sense of inquiry being evoked.

This is also the space, the element, for which I believe the final piece of Largen's chapter 3 is most relevant. What could it mean to cultivate in students a sense of enthusiasm and eagerness to continue this learning? For one thing, it means that they will enter pastoral ministry with a keen interest in supporting their communities in such interreligious relationship and learning. For another, supporting students in encountering their own agency in learning models for them—apprentices them into, in some ways—the creation of such learning opportunities for the communities in which they will lead.

Returning to the Questions
with Which We Began

So, now, what might we say by way of response to the seminary students; questions that I shared in my response to chapter 1? Let me begin by reiterating the three points: (1) meet students where they are; (2) recognize that transformative adult learning is a process of confirmation, contradiction, and continuity; and, (3) give students frames into which they can place their experience while also giving them experience to enlarge their frames.

Perhaps we can group the various questions into three rough clusters. First:

- How do we engage one another when there is nuance, contradiction, or some other form of discrepancy? I think these are important conversations to have, but we wouldn't want to step on anyone's toes, nor downgrade anyone's faith or claims.

- However, I had one woman refuse even to come to the class because she was "happy with her faith and didn't need to learn about any others." This makes me wonder, What was she really afraid of?

- Is it better to be politically correct or authentic when engaging people of other faiths? Do we worry about being offensive to a person of another faith if we are being authentic in our own?

One element that surrounds and underlies these questions is the context we inhabit, where disagreement is often perceived as personal attack, rather than as wonder leading to learning. Helping students to discover that there is a difference between "questions to persuade" and "questions to understand" is a concept which is useful in a variety of settings. One simple way to do this is to invite them to experience the difference through a practical exercise. Have students pair up, and then invite them to tell each other something they believe to be true (the world is round, chocolate is the best ice cream flavor, cats are smarter than dogs, etc.). For the first half of the time, ask them to spend five minutes, each, attempting to convince their partner that what they have confessed to be true, is *not* true, using *only* questions to do so. Pause for a few minutes of silence, and then for the second half of the time ask them to once again tell each other something they believe to be true, but this time invite them to question each other in an attempt to *understand* why that person believes it to be true.

In every instance in which I have used this exercise, students speak of finding the first mode—"questions to persuade"—an exercise that makes them feel manipulative and even deceptive, as they seek the "weak links" in a person's belief. This part of the exercise often dwindles into silence even before the time is up. The second half—"questions to understand"—on the other hand, is an experience that students report as enjoyable, and which leads them into conversations that could go on for much lengthier periods of time. In the second half, students express feelings of curiosity, wonder, sometimes even deep connection, depending on the truth being explored.

There are several such exercises available to try, found under the label of "the art of hosting," "liberating structures," or simple forms of appreciative inquiry. These are experiences that provide "rules of the game," so to speak, for helping students to contradict their taken-for-granted assumption that exploring differences must provoke defensiveness. "Questions to persuade" provoke defensiveness, "questions to understand" evoke wonder.

A second group of questions might be these:

- Is salvation a topic to set aside?

- How am I to give an account to another of the hope that is within me?

- How do we talk to other people about how we as Christians are called to relate to people of other faiths without falling into a mass of nebulous pluralism that denies any special meaning to Christianity or to the other faiths?

- How do we as Christians obey the Great Commission as recorded in Matthew 28:18-20?

- How do we strike a balance between hubris and Christian arrogance and not watering down our belief as Christians that Jesus is our only hope for atonement?

- What does it mean to us as Christians to proclaim John 14:6—"'I am the way and the truth and the life. No one comes to the Father except through me.'"

I think these questions connect with the challenge of speaking faithful truth, with a capital T, in a world moving beyond modernist certitude. Largen offers multiple ways in which to respond to these questions in her chapter 2. Here I would emphasize that these are questions that haunt multiple parts of our curricula, not solely interreligious topics. They are elements of adult faith formation that have been with us throughout the ages. The old truisms—"doubt is *not* the opposite of faith" and "certainty *is* the opposite of faith"—grow out of such dynamics. Unless we confront these questions directly, our students can graduate from seminary with crystalline philosophical commitments that never once reach deeply enough into their lives to shape their own faith, let alone provide sustenance for the difficulties of pastoral leadership in the twenty-first century.

One of the most challenging of the underlying assumptions that students bring into our classrooms is their embedded view of the authority of Scripture. The questions these students are raising either echo Scripture or quote it directly. Is it possible to hear in Scripture the living word of God, is it possible to proclaim that living word, in ways that generate wonder and belief, rather than divisiveness and judgment? Perhaps that question holds one key to its answer: the work of "wonder." As Michael Wesch makes so clear in his TED Talk "The End of Wonder," "wonder" is a state that invites questions, that connects people, that expresses our vulnerability. We have less and less practice with such experiences, and our larger cultural settings on occasion even box us away from such experiences.

 Go here to view Wesch's *The End of Wonder*.[1]

Yet engaging Scripture—and doing so across traditions, for instance, in the practice of scriptural reasoning that Largen describes—can draw students into the kind of discoveries that prompt wonder. Creating opportunities to "wonder aloud" rather than to engage in debate, to search one's own tradition at the same time someone else is searching theirs, creates an alternative process to the kind of increasingly painful public disputation that is so common.

Indeed, it may well be that it is easier to answer questions of capital "T" truth as we work with multiple faith traditions, precisely because we have more permission to "wonder" in such discussions. Many of us have found that it is more comfortable to consider differences *between* traditions than *amongst* a given tradition, that the "distal" neighbor is a more congenial place to start with than a "proximal" neighbor.

Yet that discomfort is precisely why I have found it helpful to give students frameworks from within Christianity for relating to other faith traditions. Using a heuristic such as Knitter's invites students to discover that there is diversity within Christianity about how Christians respond to other faiths, diversity that grows out of deeply held convictions which have integrity and authenticity over time. Here is a moment in which offering continuity of the sort that Robert Kegan describes becomes pertinent.

I mentioned earlier in this response some ways to approach the John 14:6 text. Here, let me note that another of the texts students often point to is the Great Commission text. Matthew 28:18-20 is often heard as "go and make disciples," as if the primary process is one of someone who is already a disciple "making" other disciples. But what if we heard that text through a different English translation, as "go and make learners"? Learning involves risking your current understanding, and going out into the world to share one's faith is likely to have as strong an impact on one's own faith as it has on anyone else's. In the Matthew text, the injunction is to go out into all the nations—surely an invitation to share and learn and grow in the midst of diversity, not to seek to erase that diversity!

---

1. QR code URL: http://www.youtube.com/watch?v=aNI2N5DPNWk.

And again, just as with the John text, it is the Holy Spirit we see in action as we share the story of Jesus with people who have never heard it before. What if the "learners" we are making are ourselves? Joyce Mercer makes the strong claim that a community without children is a dying community. Not simply because eventually it will age out and disappear, but because without children in our midst with whom to share our stories, those stories will eventually fade and perhaps become lost altogether.[2] For far too long we have heard the Great Commission text only through the lens of proselytism, rather than through the lens of learning. For all of the reasons Largen notes, engaging other faith traditions can strengthen our own faith.

Finally, there are the student's questions that come from a recognition that seminarians will be leading communities—some as pastors, some as leaders in other forms of ministry, and some from their positions in nonreligious settings:

- How can we reach and relate to "dabblers," people who have held multiple beliefs over a relatively short period of time?

- As leaders, how do we help people feel comfortable about learning and experiencing relationships with people of other religions in a way that helps them be respectful of the differences and at the same time grow in understanding and conviction about their own faith?

- What are some ways to discuss, talk, and learn about multifaith aspects in an area that could truly care less about the other in their midst in any form?

I might frame this underlying question as, In what ways can pastoral leaders be prepared to support Christian identity (their own, and others)? More than anything, please remember that people tend to teach in the ways in which they have been taught—either seeking to recapitulate such practices, or to do the opposite, depending on whether they found the pedagogy helpful or not. All three of the pedagogical points I've been making in my response to Largen are applicable here: meet students where they are; recognize that transformative adult learning is a process of confirmation, contradiction, and continuity; and, give students frames into which they can place their experience while also giving them experience to enlarge their frames. Indeed, these three phrases are not so much discontinuous intentions as they are elements of the same dynamic process. "Meeting students where they are" is the definition of Kegan's term *confirmation*. The process of giving them frames into which to put their own experience, and then experiences that enlarge those frames, is what "providing contradiction and continuity" means.

Our seminary students are not always helped by our reliance on pedagogical strategies that emphasize content at the expense of process. This is particularly true when we are working with content that touches the heart of their faith, and the faith of the communities whom they seek to lead. Especially in a world in which authority has to be built, credibility draws on perceptions of authenticity,

---

2. Joyce Mercer, *Welcoming Children: A Practical Theology of Childhood* (St. Louis: Chalice, 2005).

and personal agency lends urgency to learning, shaping our learning environments into spaces in which "obedience to truth" can be practiced becomes all the more pressing. Given that this is Parker Palmer's formulation, it is with his work that I want to conclude my response. Palmer's recent work has engaged issues of public disagreement in political spheres, and he offers a rich framework for nourishing "habits of the heart" that make democracy possible. He names five: (1) an understanding that we are all in this together, (2) an appreciation of the value of "otherness," (3) an ability to hold tension in life-giving ways, (4) a sense of personal voice and agency, and, finally, (5) a capacity to create community.[3] Teaching and learning about multiple faiths in an interreligious context offers us a rich and multivocal way to shape precisely such habits, and Largen has offered us rich ways in which to do so.

---

3. Parker Palmer, *Healing the Heart of Democracy: The Courage to Create a Politics Worthy of the Human Spirit* (San Francisco: Jossey-Bass, 2011).

Kristin Johnston Largen
Endings and Beginnings

Let me offer a final word, which I hope might serve as both and ending of the book, but also a beginning of further work, conversation, and study. To conclude, I want simply to reiterate some of the convictions that ground my own thinking, and that undergird the larger argument I have presented here. First, we live in an interreligious world: issues of religious diversity touch us all in myriad ways, and therefore facility with and an openness to other religious traditions is an absolute requirement for being a thriving and contributing member of the world community in the twenty-first century. Both institutions of higher education and religious institutions need to be much more intentional about incorporating this sort of learning in their educational formation. Second, there is not only license but even encouragement within Christian doctrine and practice itself to engage in this kind of work; and therefore interreligious teaching and learning are of critical importance for every Christian, but especially those preparing for public ministry. Finally, there are concrete strategies one can engage to implement this kind of work that have positive ramifications far beyond the immediate goals of any particular academic curriculum. Ultimately, interreligious teaching and learning isn't about the mastery of certain kinds of information, it's about the formation of certain kinds of human beings: people who understand the important role religion plays in the lives of so many people all around the world, and who want their own religious life to facilitate wonder, exploration, and hope in the face of a radically pluralistic world. One can be a faithful participant in one's own religious tradition *and* an enthusiastic participant in interreligious learning and teaching—an active member of a particular religious community as well as an active member of the larger religious neighborhood in which we all live. Dare I say, one *should* be? I do.

Works Cited

By Kristin Johnston Largen

Francis X. Clooney, S.J. *Comparative Theology: Deep Learning across Religious Borders.* Malden, MA: Wiley-Blackwell, 2010.

———. *Theology after Vedanta*: An Experiment in Comparative Theology. Albany: State University of New York Press, 1993.

Fredericks, James. "A Universal Religious Experience? Comparative Theology as an Alternative to a Theology of Religions." *Horizons* 22, no. 1 (1995): 67–87.

Griffiths, Paul J. "Indian Buddhist Meditation." In Takeuchi Yoshinori, ed. *Buddhist Spirituality: Indian, Southeast Asian, Tibetan, Early Chinese,* 34–66. New York: Crossroad, 1993.

Hodgson, Peter, and Robert King, eds.. *Christian Theology.* Newly Updated Edition. Minneapolis: Fortress Press, 1994.

Johnson, Elizabeth. *Quest for the Living God: Mapping Frontiers in the Theology of God.* New York: Continuum, 2008.

Kaltner, John. *Introducing the Qur'an for Today's Reader.* Minneapolis: Fortress Press, 2011.

Knitter, Paul. *Without Buddha I Could Not Be a Christian.* Oxford, UK: Oneworld, 2009.

Kolb, Robert, and Timothy Wengert, eds. *The Book of Concord.* Minneapolis: Fortress Press, 2000.

Largen, Kristin. *Finding God among our Neighbors: An Interreligious Systematic Theology.* Minneapolis: Fortress Press, 2013.

———. *Rethinking Salvation: What Christians Can Learn from Buddhism.* Minneapolis: Fortress Press, 2009.

Moffitt, John. "The Bhagavad Gita as a Way-Shower to the Transcendental." *Theological Studies* 38, no. 2 (June 1977): 316–31.

Palmer, Parker. *To Know as We Are Known: Education as a Spiritual Journey.* San Francisco: Harper San Francisco, 1993.

Panikkar, Raimon. *Invisible Harmony: Essays on Contemplation and Responsibility.* Harry James Cargas, ed. Minneapolis: Fortress Press, 1995.

———. *The Unknown Christ of Hinduism.* Maryknoll, NY: Orbis, 1981.

Pannenberg, Wolfhart. *Systematic Theology,* vol. 1. Geoffrey W. Bromiley, trans. Grand Rapids: Eerdmans, 1991,

Powell, Mark Allan. *Introducing the New Testament: A Historical, Literary and Theological Survey.* Grand Rapids: Baker Academic, 2009.

———. *Fortress Introduction to the Gospels.* Minneapolis: Fortress Press, 1998.

Karl Rahner. *Foundations of Christian Faith.* William Dych, trans. New York: Seabury, 1978.

Robinson, George. *Essential Judaism: A Complete Guide to Beliefs, Customs, and Rituals.* New York: Atria, 2000.

Sanneh, Lamin. *Translating the Message: The Missionary Impact on Culture.* Maryknoll, NY: Orbis, 1989.

Schoen, Robert. *What I Wish My Christian Friends Knew about Judaism*. Chicago: Loyola, 2004.

Schramm, Brooks, and Kirsi I. Stjerna. *Martin Luther, the Bible, and the Jewish People: A Reader*. Minneapolis: Fortress Press, 2012.

Sheveland, John N. "Is Yoga Religious." *Christian Century* (June 14, 2011), 22–25.

Song, C. S. *Theology from the Womb of Asia*. Maryknoll, NY: Orbis, 1986.

Thatamanil, John. *The Immanent Divine: God, Creation, and the Human Predicament*. Minneapolis: Fortress Press, 2006.

Tillich, Paul. *Christianity and the Encounter of World Religions*. Minneapolis: Fortress Press, 1994 (1963).

Sharma, Arvind, ed. *The World's Religions: A Contemporary Reader*. Minneapolis: Fortress Press, 2011.

Wells, Samuel. *Improvisation: The Drama of Christian Ethics*. Grand Rapids: Brazos, 2004.

By Mary Hess

boyd, danah. *It's Complicated: The Social Life of Networked Teens*. New Haven: Yale University Press, 2014.

Hess, Mary. "A New Culture of Learning: Digital Storytelling and Faith Formation." *Dialog* 53, no. 1 (Spring 2014): 12–22.

———. "A New Culture of Learning: Implications of Digital Culture for Communities of Faith." *Communication Research Trends* 32, no. 3 (2013): 13–20.

Ito, Mizuko, and Sonja Baumer, et al. *Hanging Out, Messing Around, and Geeking Out: Kids Living and Learning with New Media*. Cambridge: MIT Press, 2010.

Kegan, Robert. *In Over Our Heads: The Mental Demands of Modern Life*. Cambridge: Harvard University Press, 1994.

———. *The Evolving Self: Problem and Process in Human Development*. Cambridge: Harvard University Press, 1982.

Knitter, Paul. *Introducing Theologies of Religions*. Maryknoll, NY: Orbis, 2002.

McGonigal, Jane. *Reality Is Broken: Why Games Make Us Better and How They Can Change the World*. New York: Penguin, 2011.

Mercer, Joyce. *Welcoming Children: A Practical Theology of Childhood*. St. Louis: Chalice, 2005.

Palmer, Parker. *Healing the Heart of Democracy*. San Francisco: Jossey-Bass, 2011.

———. *To Know as We Are Known: Education as a Spiritual Journey*. San Francisco: HarperSanFrancisco, 1983.

Vella, Jane. *Learning to Listen, Learning to Teach*. San Francisco: Jossey-Bass, 2002.

Zull, James. *The Art of Changing the Brain: Enriching the Practice of Teaching by Exploring the Biology of Learning*. Sterling, Va.: Stylus, 2002.

By Christy Lohr Sapp

Francisco, Adam. *Martin Luther and Islam: A Study in Sixteenth-Century Polemics and Apologetics*. Leiden: Brill. 2007.

Heckman, Bud, and Rori Picker Neiss, eds. *InterActive Faith: The Essential Interreligious Community-Building Handbook*. Woodstock, VT: Skylight Paths, 2008.

Hick, John. *An Interpretation of Religion*. New Haven: Yale University Press, 1989.

Sapp, Lohr. "Obama's Interfaith Service Challenge: A Call for a New Theology of Service in American Higher Education." *Dialog* 50, no. 3 (Fall 2011): 280–88.

Lonsdale, Akasha. *Do I Kneel or Do I Bow? What You Need to Know When Attending Religious Occasions.* London: Kuperard, 2010.

Magida, Arthur, and Stuart Matlins, eds. *How to Be a Perfect Stranger: The Essential Religious Etiquette Handbook.* 4th ed. Woodstock, VT: SkyLight Paths, 2006.

MacIntyre, Alisdair. *Which Justice? Whose Rationality?* Notre Dame, IN: University of Notre Dame Press, 1988.

Peace, Jennifer Howe, Or Rose, and Gregory Mobley, eds. *My Neighbor's Faith: Stories of Interreligious Encounter, Growth, and Transformation.* Maryknoll, NY: Orbis, 2012.

Prothero, Stephen. *Religious Literacy: What Every American Needs to Know—and Doesn't.* New York: HarperOne, 2007.

Roozen, David, and Heidi Hadsell, eds. *Changing the Way Seminaries Teach: Pedagogies for Interfaith Dialogue.* Hartford: Hartford Seminary, 2009.

Schweizer, Mark. *The Baritone Wore Chiffon: A Liturgical Mystery.* Hopkinsville, KY: St. James Music Press, 2004.

Stendahl, Krister. "Remarks Upon Receipt of the 1996 Rabbi Marc Tanenbaum Award." *Journal of Ecumenical Studies* 34, no. 3 (Summer 1997): 455.